Teens' Guide to Making Friends

Make Friends With Confidence, Navigate Awkward Situations, and Why Mistakes Aren't the End of the World

PickWood Publishing

Teens' Guide Series

Also by Kev Chilton

TEENS' GUIDE TO MAKING FRIENDS

Teens' Guide Book Series

https://kevchilton.com/books

https://kevchilton.com/books

as a result of the use of the information contained within this document, including, but not limited to, errors, omissions, or inaccuracies.

Dedication

With thanks to Beth, whose initial conversations gave me the idea to create this five-book series.

A special thanks to Grace for her meticulous research and invaluable advice, which played a pivotal role in creating each book.

To my good friend, Anna, who kept me sane throughout!

Contents

Introduction

B EING A TEENAGER CAN be one of the most exciting times of your life. You're going through an extraordinary amount of changes—physical and emotional—much like a caterpillar becoming a butterfly. Only, you don't get to hide away in a chrysalis while they happen. You have to deal with the outside world and all its expectations, judgements, and stresses. All these issues are much easier to deal with if you have a loyal group of friends by your side.

But what if making those friends is part of the stress? You're not alone. Lots of teenagers struggle with making friends, keeping friends, and feeling worthy of friends. It's a normal part of adolescence that you might grow apart from the friends you had as a child, but that doesn't mean the next group is waiting in the wings, ready to take over.

Teenage friendships, when they happen, tend to forge quickly, which doesn't help if you're standing on the sidelines. It looks effortless for others, so why not for you?

The obvious answer must be because there is something wrong with you. Everyone else can see it and they keep away. No matter how many times you're told otherwise by the grown ups around you, you remain convinced that you've been judged and deemed unworthy by your peers.

I'm here to show you why that is not the case. In fact, it is a side effect of puberty that your brain becomes a self-saboteur, projecting your own insecurities onto others. What you're imagining is not their opinions, but your own, whether conscious or subconscious. The internet is full of tips about how to meet people, but without addressing issues with self-esteem and self-confidence, you're not going to make meaningful connections. It's only by really being comfortable with yourself that you'll find your people.

Teens are biologically programmed to want to make social connections with others and, under the right conditions, making friends is easy and natural. Often, being unable to make friends is symptomatic of something else getting in the way. That could be anxiety about speaking to new people, an overwhelming fear of rejection, or even the fact that you just don't get out enough. Rather than recycling the same old advice like "just be yourself" or "you're not smiling enough," in these pages, you will find simple exercises to help you overcome your anxieties, scientific explanations to understand why you care so much about the opinions of others, and practical advice on building up your self-esteem.

Change Comes From Within

Your brain has a few windows in its life where it can learn new things much more easily. Learning your first language after the age of eight is nearly impossible, which is why so much emphasis is placed on communication in elementary school. Adolescence opens the brain's second window for rapid and intensive learning. According to research compiled by UNICEF, this window focuses on developments in "sensation seeking, motivation for social relations, and sensitivity to social evaluation" (UNICEF, 2018). Basically, that means that how you approach social situations and how you respond to other people is explored while you're a teenager. And what your brain learns now sets the baseline for the rest of your life. This means that withdrawing from social situations all together isn't like waiting for the storm to be over. Without making those vital neural connections now, you'll be living in the storm forever.

More and more, as we go through life, we find ourselves in situations that we have little to no control over: speaking in public, navigating crowded rooms, interacting with strangers, or meeting new people for example. Some of these situations will make you feel awkward, uncomfortable, and anxious even if you've navigated them a hundred times before. By learning the best ways to overcome your anxieties and have successful interactions at an age where you have more control over your degree of exposure, you are setting yourself up for continued success.

It might feel like you're alone in finding things difficult, but the reality is that more people suffer with anxiety and confidence issues than you could ever imagine. But by using strategies like those found in this book, they are able to step outside of their comfort zones and handle difficult situations that they once would have seen themselves hiding from. Celebrities like Adele, Jennifer Lawrence, Kristen Bell, Chris Evans, and Finn Wolfhard have all gone public with their own stories and experiences detailing their struggles in order to show people just like you that there is a light at the end of the tunnel.

Everyone's in it Together

The hardest thing to remember is that everyone going through adolescence feels some of the same things as you. Everyone has something that's changed about their body that makes them feel uncomfortable. Everyone is struggling with unpredictable emotions and the effect they are having on relationships with friends and caregivers. Everyone is more aware of how other people see them, and that is going to affect how they behave in public. Some people are confident and others aren't, but you can't always tell who is who by their behavior. Often, the people who shout the loudest have the lowest self-esteem.

Your social history and your personality come into play much more now than they have in the past. If you've experienced rejection before, you're going to be more cautious approaching new people than someone who has never been hurt. Some people will find making friends easier than others, but that doesn't mean you are a lost cause. It might take you a bit longer than others, or you might experience more false starts and rejections, but I promise you, everyone can make those vital human connections.

You'll notice that throughout this book I use the term "caregiver" to refer to an adult who is responsible for the care of someone under the age of 18. Modern families come in many different forms and I think it's important to acknowledge this. The term "caregiver" includes, but is not limited to, birth parents, foster parents, adoptive parents, grandparents, aunts, uncles, older siblings who have taken on legal guardianship, social workers, and adults employed by children's homes.

When It All Goes Wrong

I've spent my life working as an inner city cop, which means I've interviewed just about every type of person there is. I had to be good at forming relationships quickly, whether it was with someone who needed help or with a suspect I was interviewing. Essentially, I got really good at making friends, but that wasn't always the case. I'm going to share with you the moment from my childhood that I still regret to this day, the reason why I lost all my confidence and stopped trying to talk to people at school. Why? Because I want to show that making a mistake in high school, although it feels awful, doesn't have to kill off your social life or your confidence.

In my mid-teens, sitting in a classroom with 34 other kids, I decided to tell a joke. That sounds fairly innocuous, but the situation quickly escalated. I was feeling cocky and overconfident, and that, combined with my desire to be liked by my peers, convinced me that this was exactly what I needed to do to cement my popularity. I had images in my head of them laughing so hard they fell from their desks and were left rolling on the floor. People would pass me in the corridor and ask me to tell it again, patting me on the back and commending me for my amazing sense of humor.

Oh, how far from reality those thoughts were. Once all eyes had turned to me, I panicked. What if they didn't think it was funny? What if they laughed at me because I liked a stupid joke? I would never hear the end of it. Instead of clapping me in the corridors, the entire school would point at me and whisper about the boy who thought he was funny.

The end of the joke made a quick exit from my brain and I was left with nothing to offer the class except my wide-eyed stare. My tongue swelled and my mouth ran drier than the Sahara desert. I could feel the sweat gathering on my forehead and my cheeks felt so hot, I was half expecting to spontaneously combust. The silence stretched on for what felt like hours, but in fact, it was only about five seconds. Five seconds that completely stripped me of my self-confidence and ensured that I didn't put my hand up again in class for years.

I wish someone had taken me aside and told me that, in reality, the majority of the class would forget it ever happened by the end of the week. That every time I thought I caught someone talking about me, they were most likely discussing something completely different. That the way to make friends is not by showing off what you think they want to see, but instead by being the best version of your true self that you can be.

You're already a step ahead of me. Whatever experiences you've had that have led you here are no longer going to define your adolescence. You've sought help because you want to make some changes and you're not going to let anxiety, low self-esteem, and negative social interactions rule your life. By picking up this book, you've already made the first step on the path to greater confidence, positive social experiences, and fulfilling friendships. Let's move on to the next.

ESPECIALLY FOR YOU!

https://kevchilton.com/free-books

FREE BOOKS

Specially prepared books for
teens and adults...

https://kevchilton.com/free-books

Chapter One

It's Official: Adolescence Sucks!

*A*DOLESCENCE IS JUST ONE *big walking pimple.* –Carol Burnett

Being a teenager is supposed to encompass some of the best years of your life, at least according to the adults who know what's on the other side. Okay, so you're still at school, and now you've got the added pressure of exams to navigate, but you're also handed extra independence and the freedom to take more control over your own life and your own decisions. Your responsible adults might get involved more than you want, but there's a definite shift in expectations from both parties.

As a kid, this is probably something you were looking forward to. Growing up sounds exciting and there are loads of things to look forward to. So why is the reality such a disappointment? Luckily, we can sum up the problem in one word: puberty. While you're busy looking forward to spending more time hanging out with your mates, dipping a tentative toe into the dating pool, and having a curfew with double figures, your hormones seem to be directly plotting against you.

Biology Is a Bitch

You might think you know exactly what happens to your body when you go through adolescence; after all, most school curriculums cover it repeatedly. What they don't always tell you, though, is what's going on behind the scenes.

Let the Change Begin!

Everyone starts puberty at a different age. Most people start to feel changes between the ages of 8 and 14. Once your body hits its own personal point-of-no-return, your brain releases an entirely new hormone into your bloodstream. This hormone is called GnRH—scientific name gonadotropin-releasing hormone—and it's basically chaos personified. (Dowshen, 2015). Once it makes its way to your sexual organs, it causes them to start behaving differently. If you have ovaries, they'll begin to manufacture estrogen, and if you have testes, they'll manufacture more testosterone. Both these hormones are responsible for the physical changes you'll see in your bodies, but they also have a substantial effect on the way that you feel and how you process your emotions.

Growth Spurt or Sprouting Growths?

During puberty your entire body speeds up its growth rate. Some people can grow as much as 4 in taller in a year, but it's not just your height that is changing. You'll gain weight as your body starts to develop muscle mass and fat stores. (Dowshen, 2015). This is perfectly normal, but it can make you feel uncomfortable and self-conscious because it's an obvious change that other people can see. As if growing out of your clothes almost overnight wasn't enough cause for embarrassment, getting used to your new body dimensions can take a while. Some teenagers find they become clumsier during puberty, because their limbs are slightly different lengths, or they didn't realize they now have to duck through doorways.

Another change that everyone can see is that you'll start to grow more body hair. Everyone has a thin covering of hair on their arms and legs, but once those puberty hormones kick in, this hair can become darker and thicker, and it starts to grow from new places, like under your arms and around your groin.

The changing hormone levels also affect your skin. Some people find their skin gets drier; others find it is more oily. Most teenagers suffer from acne at some point during puberty. Acne most often appears on your face, but it can also break out on your back, shoulders, and chest.

Your Brain Is a Saboteur

The effect that increased estrogen and testosterone have on your bodies is nothing compared to how they can mess up your brain. During puberty, your brain is completely rewired as you level up from a child's brain to an adult's. Until now, your thoughts have been fairly simple; I'm hungry, I want to play football, that child looks friendly. But once puberty strikes, you start to become more aware of other people and their opinions. You also become more aware of your own looks, actions, and behavior, especially in the context of how other people view you.

Here's an example:

You wear your comfiest t-shirt and jeans to the cinema to meet some friends. Some other teens from your class are there too, but they are significantly more dressed up. You don't really know them but give a small wave and a smile to be polite. The group laughs, turns around, and walks off.

So, how do you feel?

In all probability, they didn't see you and were laughing at something one of them said. But give your brain a big dose of crazy puberty hormones and it goes into overdrive.

Are they laughing at me? Is it my clothes, my hair, my skin, or just because they hate me? I shouldn't have waved; waving is lame and now they think I'm lame. They're going to tell everyone at school what a loser I am and the whole school will laugh at me. I can't go in tomorrow. Maybe I'd better just transfer.

During adolescence, your brain learns to analyze situations, which is basically it playing a giant game of "What if?" Instead of shrugging and moving on, you start imagining an endless stream of scenarios, which can quickly lead to extreme "solutions." Teenagers have a reputation for overreacting and being dramatic, but you can't actually help it! It's all part of growing up and developing a proper adult brain. Eventually your brain works out what is an appropriate amount of analyzing in situations like these and you'll stop feeling like a crazy person, but until then, you'll have to put up with watching your friends overthink every situation just as badly as you do.

Even the Good Bits Suck

We've already established that adolescence is the time when your body goes haywire and your brain betrays you, so it would make sense to lie low for five or six years until it all blows over, right? Unfortunately, life doesn't work that way, and many of the changes you're going through rely on social interactions to fine-tune them.

Imagine you've invented a new kind of ice cream. You need people to taste it to see if they like it. The first person says it's too sweet, so you change the recipe. The next person says it's too fruity, so you change it again. You repeat the process until eventually everyone says they love it, even if that takes a year. Now, imagine you spend that year developing your ice cream in secret with only you tasting it and then launch it in the world. Will it be as well received?

In case you didn't work it out, you're the ice cream. Not that you should spend your teenage years asking people to lick you; you're a metaphorical ice cream. Every social interaction, every boundary you push, and every new friend you make contributes to the well-rounded adult you will become. Even though everything feels awkward at the time, it's necessary to make the best version of you.

During your teenage years, you will have many wonderful experiences, and you will remember those far better than the horrible ones, even if it doesn't seem like it right now. This is the time of your life when you start to forge deeper and more meaningful friendships with people you choose because you're on the same path, rather than because your parents are friends or you live nearby.

For the first time, you're capable of forming informed opinions and preferences. These can range from which books you like to which people are worth hanging out with. You also start to make long-term plans, which are more grounded in reality, and you consider where you belong in society. You'll also have more independence over making your own decisions, and for the first time have to deal with serious consequences of making the wrong ones. Your adolescence is the time to start trying out new activities, new personal styles, and really working out exactly who you are. All while dealing with the clumsiest, spottiest, least confident version of yourself. What could possibly go wrong?

What Can You Do About it?

It's all very well knowing what is happening to you, but that doesn't mean you can do much to control it. Those hormones are going to have their way with you, whether you like it or not, but what you do have agency over is how you manage those changes and the unpredictability they bring. Here are a few suggestions for making the road through puberty as smooth as you can.

Self-Care Begins at Home

Dealing with growth spurts and rapid brain development requires your body to consume an enormous amount of energy. If you've been feeling sleepy, sluggish, and lacking the get-up-and-go that children seem to have in abundance, this is why.

Many teenagers use the weight gained through puberty as a reason to start dieting, but this is actually giving your body less energy to do what it needs to do. A balanced diet with regular meals and plenty of vegetables—because they're full of the vitamins you need to support bone and muscle growth—will make sure your energy stores are replenished regularly. You might be craving junk food, but that's only because extracting calories from sugar is the fastest way for your body to get energy, and once it's burned through it, you'll end up feeling flat again.

Another way to combat that sluggish feeling is to make sure you get some regular exercise. Exercise makes you feel better because it releases endorphins in your brain and these lift your mood and slow down the production of stress hormones, including adrenaline and cortisol. Go for a walk, dance to your top playlist, learn a yoga routine, or join a team sport.

Exercise also helps to clear your mind, so if you've had an argument or found a situation particularly stressful, this is a great way to calm down.

Another way to reduce the hormones that raise your stress levels is to try some meditation exercises. You can download some simple exercises or check out YouTube for guided meditation that will help you regulate your breathing and relax your muscles.

Alternatively, listening to some slow music in a darkened room, having a soak in the bath with an audiobook, or taking a walk through nature are all other good ways to relieve stress.

An Exercise in Relaxation

Not sure where to start? Try this set of breathing exercises to help you calm down and refocus in just five minutes.

1. Make sure you're somewhere quiet where you won't be disturbed. This won't work if you get halfway through and your annoying little brother appears with a Nerf gun. Settle into a comfortable position; either lying down or sitting somewhere relaxed is best.

2. Close your eyes and breath in slowly through your nose as you count one, two, and three.

3. Hold your breath for the same amount of time. Don't be tempted to count faster; you won't suffocate unless you have the lung capacity of a field mouse.

4. Breathe out through your mouth. You have two options here and both work well. You can either breathe out slowly for a count of three or expel the entire breath out in one short, sharp huff.

5. As you get more practice at deep breathing, you can change the inhale/exhale count to five.

Chapter Two

Why Don't Grown Ups Have a Clue?

ONE OF THE CRUELTIES of teenage hood is that you'll never know what your parents were really like at your age, and they'll never accurately remember. –Una LaMarche

As a teenager, your relationship with your caregivers also enters a period of turmoil. Hopefully, once you reach adulthood, it will have developed into a strong bond based on mutual respect, but during adolescence, it can feel like a battle of good vs evil. In this movie, the tyrannical bad guys (them) seek to constantly thwart the hormone-riddled hero (you) at every turn by sapping their fun, interfering with their lives, and insisting on some arcane torture known as "studying." But, at the end of the movie, there's a grand twist: The villain was once an independence-seeking teen too. Imagine the shock!

You'll Never See Eye to Eye

What happens in adulthood that makes it so difficult to relate to teenagers? In part, we've already answered that; it's hormones and brain development. An adult, with a fully developed brain that isn't controlled by the hormones of puberty, is a "big picture" kind of thinker. They are fully aware of their place in the world, what they need to do to maintain—or improve—it, and have become really good at analyzing how events are going to effect them. Most adults will have a disagreement with a friend and know that, in the grand scheme of things, it isn't going to be the end of the world. Both parties are capable of resolving their issues and moving on.

What adults are not very good at doing, is remembering how things were different when they were teenagers. See, you know that a disagreement with a friend actually could be the end of the world as you know it. That friend might be the only support you have in a subject you hate at school, and if they're not talking to you, that class gets a whole lot scarier. Falling out with this particular friend might mean you have no one to sit next to on the bus, leaving that open space to be occupied by anyone, and you can't cope with the unpredictability of that situation.

You could be worried that they'll turn on you and reveal all your biggest secrets to the class, or you might just be upset because they said something that hurt you and you're no longer sure if you can trust them.

The problem here is that, in these scenarios, both adult and teenager know they are right, and therefore, both fail to see how the other side can also be right. However, what the adult fails to take into account is that the teenager is coming from a very different place than them, and so their adult perspective doesn't take into account the teenager's smaller world, heightened emotional state, or other worries. It's like someone from Mexico complaining about a cold day to someone from Canada. It's cold to them, even if it isn't actually that cold in general.

The Great Generational Divide

Teenagers now live in a vastly different time compared to when their caregivers were teenagers. Social media didn't exist until the early 2000s, and even then, it was nowhere near as impactful on everyone's lives as it is now. There were households who didn't have internet and not everyone had a mobile phone. But rather than adding new situations for teens to deal with, they have amplified those that have plagued them for decades. Gossip has always spread, teens have always been concerned with fitting in, and peer pressure has always been at the root of a hundred bad decisions.

The point here is that your problems are not new; they are just new to you. The large number of teenagers who feel that their caregivers won't understand their problems fail to take into account that they once had the same issues—even if it feels like it was back in the dark ages.

Do as I Say, Not as I Did!

I'm sorry to have to say this, but there are actually a lot of good reasons to listen to the grown ups in your life. They've made it through the other side of adolescence and can use the wonderful skill of hindsight to look back on their teenage years and cringe at all the awful choices they made. They're now living with the consequences of not studying enough, falling in love with the wrong person, and wearing flannel shirts and scrunchies. And believe it or not, the reason they are so fond of handing out advice and telling you what to do, is because they're trying to prevent you from making the same mistakes. Especially with flannel shirts. And I guarantee that they didn't listen to their parents either. It's a perpetual cycle.

Learn a Common Language

What stops you talking to your caregivers about something important? Here are a few common answers that seem to cover most situations:

- I don't want them to be disappointed in me and my choices.

- They won't understand. They've never been in this situation.

- They'll ask too many questions.

- They always tell me not to make such a big deal of things.

- My friend asked their parents and got yelled at; why would mine do anything differently?

- It's too embarrassing to discuss.

If any of those seem familiar, now might be a good time to show this chapter to your grown ups. Leave it open somewhere they might find it, like under the tv remote, next to the kettle, or in their most comfortable slippers. Because getting adults and teenagers talking constructively is really important. It helps your cognitive development, can inspire better decision making, and improves your relationship. Teenagers who feel supported at home are more confident outside of it.

Grown Ups, Time to Open Up

The key to good intergenerational communication is openness. That doesn't mean you spill every secret and lay yourself bare, rather the questions you ask should be open-ended. Open-ended questions allow for interpretation and give people the chance to focus on the issues that are bothering them. They also don't have a right answer, which takes away any anxiety people might feel about getting it wrong. Here's an example of a typical conversation with close-ended questions, which a lot of caregivers ask at the end of a school day:

Caregiver: Did you have a good day today?

Teen: Yeah

Caregiver: Did you get your science test result back?

Teen: Yeah

Caregiver: And?

Teen: 70%

Caregiver: That sounds like it could have been better.

Teen: Whatever.

I bet you've had a similar chat this week. Notice how the teen has a limited scope for answering. Sure, they could elaborate if they wanted to, but that would be down to them. Open-ended questions draw longer responses by default. Here's the same topic of conversation again, but this time with open-ended questions from the caregiver.

Caregiver: How was your day?

Teen: It was ok. I had art, which I like, but the English lesson was boring because I've already finished the book. Oh, and Mr. Scott gave our science tests back.

Caregiver: Oh yeah? Tell me about it.

Teen: I got 70%. At first I panicked cos I think that's my worst mark yet, but when we went through it in class I realized I only actually messed up one section. And a few other kids did the same so we've made plans to go through it this weekend.

Caregiver: Sounds like a good plan. Well done.

Spot the difference? Open-ended questions allow for more input, but that's not just it. This teen got a chance to talk about their test score without being judged by their caregiver. In fact, they actually got praised for making a good decision, which will encourage them to open up in the future. It's a much more positive experience.

Teen-Led Understanding

As a teen, there are times when you'll have to initiate conversations with caregivers, which you might find difficult or uncomfortable. It doesn't matter the topic, if you're worried you'll get one of the above negative responses, you'll probably find yourself putting it off. Remind your adults that they need to see things from your perspective and let you explain the situation without making their own judgements. Here are a few conversation starters:

- I need to tell you how I feel about something. Please remember that this is important to me, even if it doesn't seem important to you.

- Something has happened and I need your advice so I can make a good choice. I can't change what's in the past, so let's start from where we are now.

- I want to ask you about something. Please don't make any assumptions or jump to conclusions.

Yeah, okay, they might sound a bit clunky and like they're straight out of a therapist's textbook, but sometimes when you're talking to grown ups, you need to put things really clearly for them. Often, the fact that you're talking to them at all, without stomping, grunting, or screaming, "it's not fair!" is enough to get them to shut up and listen.

Where to Find a Trusted Adult

If, for whatever reason, you still don't feel like you can talk to your caregivers about something important, there are other places you can turn to. It's so important to feel supported when you have difficult decisions and life choices to make, whether you're dealing with pressure to try drugs, bullying, questioning your identity, teenage pregnancy, or any other number of potentially serious situations. These resources will help you find someone who will listen to you and provide confidential advice. If they need to inform anyone else about what you've told them, they will let you know beforehand.

Adults You Know

Teachers or other adults in school are a great resource if you need someone to chat to, and most are always willing to listen. Pick someone you feel you have a good relationship with. That could be your form teacher, subject teacher, coach, librarian, or teaching assistant.

Any adult you have a relationship with outside of school, if they work or volunteer with children, will have a vested interest in your wellbeing. Sports coaches or scout leaders can often tell when something is troubling you better than other adults because they work more closely and more informally with the kids in their groups. Religious leaders are also a great source of comfort and advice, especially if you know them well from attending youth groups at your place of worship.

Phone Lines and Services

If you feel more comfortable talking anonymously, there are several phone lines and text messaging services you can contact where trained volunteers will be able to give you help and support. A more comprehensive list will be available at the end of this book.

Anyone can make an appointment at their local sexual health clinic, even those who are under 16. They offer free and confidential, non-judgemental support to young people without needing to involve their caregivers.

For advice on anything, if you are in the UK, you can call Childline at 0800 1111 or access their online message boards at . US readers can call the Boys Town National Hotline on 1-800-448-1300 or text the word "VOICE" to their textline, which is 20121.

For information on anything to do with drugs, visit or text 82111 in the UK.

If you need to discuss anything relating to your mental health or need immediate help because you are feeling depressed or having suicidal thoughts, UK readers can text "YoungMinds" on 85258. You can find more support at . US readers can text "Crisis" on 741741

Chapter Three

Making Friends is Hard Sometimes

*F*RIENDSHIP IS SO WEIRD. *You just pick a human you've met and you're like, 'Yep, I like this one,' and you just do stuff with them.* –Bill Murray

Who Needs Friends?

Short answer; everyone! Even some animals in the wild form friendship groups that are separate from their family groups. Recent studies have shown that chimpanzees, zebras, dolphins, elephants, squirrels, and even some birds actively choose to spend time with their friends over other creatures (Hooper et al., 2022). Animals select their friends by looking for similarities. They might be a similar age, enjoy hunting in the same area, or even have the same temperament.

We take it for granted that friendship is part of our life, but where did the notion come from and why does it work? On a biological level, it has been proven that being with friends has a massive, positive effect on your brain chemistry. Socializing with people we like and trust produces the big three "happy hormones" in your brain: serotonin, dopamine, and oxytocin. (Mandel, 2017). If you could synthesize the feeling of happiness, those would be the main ingredients, and when we're happy, we want to do more of whatever makes us feel that way. This is why we make friends and keep spending time with them.

But spending time with your friends can have other health benefits as a result of these chemicals zipping around in your brain. Friends support us and our bodies know this, so when friends are around, we feel less stressed. This is why you feel better working on a school project with your friend rather than a random partner. We trust our friends; they are predictable and they know how we like to be helped. This is the same reason why strangers can feel threatening and scary: You don't know what they're going to do and your teenage brain starts imagining all the bad things they'll do to you if you talk to them.

But without getting over this hurdle and talking to strangers, you can't make any friends, and unless you've picked up this book by mistake, that's something you're eager to do. You've probably convinced yourself that making friends is something that everyone else finds easy, but the reality is that they're all going through the same chemical processes inside their brain. It's just that some people react more strongly to the anxiety messages than others.

Define Friendship

We choose our friends in a similar way to the animals—you prefer to spend time with people you have something in common with. As a child, you're usually happy to play with whoever is there, but as you reach adolescence you become much more discerning. You enjoy hanging out with someone if you have a conversation about a topic you're both interested in. You'll enjoy doing the same things, like playing sports or video games, watching horror films, or volunteering together.

Good friends also introduce us to positive new experiences and support us while we learn. Maybe you and your friend bonded because you both play musical instruments, and now they're also teaching you to rollerblade. People are much more likely to try a new activity and stick with it if they have a friend with them.

You'll notice I used the phrase "good friends" in the previous paragraph. This was deliberate because you can have bad friends too, and I don't mean the ones who forget to like your Instagram post and always cancel plans at the last minute. You see, friendships as a teenager are a lot more complicated than they were when you were a child, and friends come in all sorts of shapes and sizes.

Signs of a Bad Friend

If you find it difficult to make friends and only have a small social circle, it can be really hard to sever ties with someone, even if hanging out with them makes you feel depressed and unworthy. Many people justify sticking with bad friends because they argue that any friends are better than no friends. But would you keep eating food that made you sick? No, you'd look for something better. You'd probably rather eat nothing at all. Bad friends are like food poisoning, but with the right treatment, you can get them out of your system.

Good friends are enjoyable to be around, but bad friends can feel exhausting because they take more from the relationship than they give. If you find yourself avoiding a message from someone because you know you'll have to deal with some sort of drama yet again, it's probably worth evaluating that friendship. Are they just going through a bad phase at the moment, or have they always used you as their support but never returned the favor? Friendship should be a two-way street, and if you feel like you're always playing the same role in the relationship, it's time to let it go.

Bad friends often seek to make themselves look or feel better by putting you down. They're subtle about it, so you don't notice it as much as you would notice negative comments from a bully. Remember, friends should encourage you and lift you up; if you have one who constantly criticizes your outfit, your suggestions, or your choices in general, they're not worth your time.

Sometimes bad friends aren't malicious, but they can be irresponsible. They encourage bad behaviors, pressure you to do things that make you uncomfortable, and mock you if you resist. During adolescence, these typically involve drugs, alcohol, sexual behavior, and petty crimes like shoplifting. But it doesn't have to be that serious; bad friends could also encourage you to skip class, interrupt your studies, and even be rude to your other friends.

Another type of bad friend is one who doesn't respect your boundaries or your wishes. Respect is a key part of any relationship, and if you've asked someone not to do something, they should do as they're asked. Bad friends insert themselves into your plans, turn up unannounced, and copy your achievements. Every time you get something new, do they suddenly have the same item the following week? They're not letting you be yourself, and they're trying to keep the attention on them.

It's not just important to spot the bad friends who are attaching themselves to you; you also need to make sure it isn't you who is being a bad friend. Evaluating your own behavior is a really difficult skill, but it's a really important one to learn. If you are worrying because a friend has been distant lately, could it be because they consider you a bad friend and are trying to end the relationship? No one likes to hear that they've been doing something wrong, especially if that resulted in hurting a friend. But if you've spotted some of your own actions in this section, don't worry. Everyone going through adolescence is still learning. If you know what the problem is, you can change it.

Healthy Friendships

A healthy friendship should be based on mutual respect for each other and your differences. Respect is a word that gets thrown around a lot when talking about teenagers, usually in the context of them not respecting grown ups. You've probably never bothered to look the word up in the dictionary, but there are a few slightly different meanings of respect that are worth clarifying.

You can respect someone because you admire them or because they have done something amazing. Children respect adults because they are taught that being a grown up is something special and they are wise creatures who should be listened to. As you get older, you'll realize this isn't always the case, which is when people start complaining that teenagers are being disrespectful.

Often teenagers mistake this kind of respect for another kind, which is based on a mutual liking for each other. They try to initiate friendships with kids they admire; the popular girl, the best sportsman, or someone with rich parents for example. These friendships aren't built on an even ground and are very rarely sustainable.

Respect between friends starts with simply acknowledging that your friend has their own thoughts, feelings, preferences, and hobbies. Within a healthy friendship both people should be able to express their own personalities equally. These friendships are built on common ground and the fact that both people like each other. Further on in this chapter, we'll look at some ways you can put yourself in the right situation to find these people.

How to Be a Good Friend

Teenage friendships are different from any relationship you will have had so far. They are felt more deeply and often are placed in a higher regard than family relationships, because as we've already seen, no one can understand what you're going through as well as someone your own age. Those who have had good relationships with their caregivers, siblings, extended family, and other children before they hit adolescence aren't guaranteed to make friends easily as teenagers. Neither are those who come from difficult circumstances guaranteed to struggle. The changes that hit you during puberty affect everyone differently and having had good friendships in the past might help you recognize good friendships in the future.

As adolescents, you will support each other through a whole range of new experiences, including first loves and sexual experiences, exam stress, bullying, introductions to alcohol and possibly drugs, and disagreements with family. That's just the standard set; I haven't even thrown in some of the more difficult things that teenagers shouldn't have to deal with, like bereavement, gang pressure, teenage pregnancy, and any form of abuse. As your friends are usually the first level of support, that mutual respect is really important. It feels awful when your friends don't respond the way you need them to. Good friends make everything easier. They are fun to spend time with and won't always insist on doing what they want. They will laugh with you instead of at you and will listen to your problems rather than just burdening you with theirs. It's not always easy to be a good friend, but it is incredibly rewarding.

Once you've started to increase your social circle, you'll want to make sure you're being a good friend to those around you. Here are some of the basics on how to do so:

- Listen. And I mean, really listen. Imagine you're going to be taking a pop quiz later and you'll need to remember everything they said. In fact, back in the early days of the internet, sending your friends a "how well do you know me?" quiz was a very popular activity—heaven forbid you and your BFF didn't score 100% on each others'. Whether your friend is telling you about something they enjoy or something that's troubling them, show them that you respect them by taking time to be interested in their activities.

- Be Supportive. We're all different; we like different things and different people. Even when you have friends that you share a lot of common activities and personality traits with, there will be times you think they're doing something stupid. But you don't always have to tell them—unless it's something dangerous or illegal, in which case you can absolutely weigh in with your opinion and some cold, hard facts. Being judged or put down by someone you respect feels awful because you put a lot of weight in their opinion. You might not like the person they have a crush on, you might think their Pokémon card collection is babyish, or you might think their new hairstyle isn't flattering. But if they're happy with their choices, a good friend should support them, rather than criticize.

- Be Loyal. Good friends stick up for each other, even when the other person isn't there. You should never talk about anything your friend has told you in private with other people, even if that person also knows. This includes their caregivers or teachers, even if you think they have a right to know. Instead, encourage your friend to speak up by themselves and offer to be there to hold their hand—literally or metaphorically—when they do.

- Have fun. Doing something you enjoy is twice as fun when you do it with your friends, and the chances are you've become friends because you have a shared interest in common. So go ahead and throw a weekly movie night, wear out your shoes window shopping, drink hot chocolate and eat donuts 'til you feel like you're going to explode! It's so easy to forget, now that everyone has a cell phone and you can be in constant contact, that there are activities that fuel a friendship, not just words. Make sure you make time for each other in the real world and outside of school if possible. After all, that's where all the fun stuff happens anyway.

Common Problems and How to Overcome Them

There is some spectacularly bad advice floating around out there about how to make friends, advice that makes it seem like everyone else finds it easy and you need to change yourself or risk becoming a hermit in the future. Have you heard any of these before?

- "You need to be more outgoing!"

- "Smile more. You don't look friendly."

- "Just go talk to people. They won't bite."

- "You'll never make friends your own age if you don't do what everyone else is doing."

I have to admit, I cringed just writing them. It felt like high school all over again. Although well-meaning, each piece of advice judges you for doing something wrong. They all assume that there's a good reason why people aren't lining up to befriend you, but they also make it sound incredibly easy to change that.

Here's the plain truth for you: Will you have to change something in order to make the friends you deserve? Probably. Will it be easy? Probably not. Will it be worth it? Yes. And here's the big one: Will it be an intrinsic part of your personality? Absolutely not! There is nothing wrong with you, and there is nothing about you that people are not going to love. They just don't know it yet because they haven't had a chance to see you for the wonderful, amazing, totally unique person that you are. And that's what we have to change.

Without altering your personality, I am going to show you how changing some of your behaviors can make you more open to friendship, and the first step is to look at what is causing the problem in the first place.

I Never Meet Anyone

I've talked incessantly about friendships starting because people have a common interest, but what if your interests and passions are completely different to the other teens you meet? It happens, especially when people live in smaller communities. An average-sized public high school probably has around 500–600 students divided across the years. The largest public high school in the US has more than 14,000 students registered, and the smallest public high schools have fewer than 10 (Public School Review, 2022). What if you're homeschooled? Your pool of potential friends is even smaller.

A good place to meet like-minded people is to find where they hang out and go there. Is there a school or a community club that you would enjoy? Most high schools have a wide range of sports clubs (e.g.: drama, singing, dancing, art, all manner of different bands, book clubs, LGBT+ clubs, etc.) and if there isn't one, could you start one? High schools love it when students take initiative, so if you want to start an anime appreciation society, retro gamers club, or green gardening club, they will support you. You never know how many other people out there will be interested unless you try. The same is true of community groups. Your local library probably has a list of what's on, as will your place of worship, community hall, and town website or Facebook page.

Another perfectly valid place to meet like-minded people is online. Yes, there are well-publicized dangers with connecting with people online who you don't know. Social media pages are unverified and might not actually belong to the person in the photos. But there are other places where you can meet people where they have less incentive to hide behind a fake facade. Remember to never give out personal information or agree to meet anyone in real life unless you have video chatted online first so you know they are who they say they are.

If you're a fan of online video games, you can meet and chat to other players while gaming online. Many online friendships have started this way because you all know one thing you have in common and you get a good hit of dopamine while doing it. This makes you want to do it again and associates everyone involved in the experience with the feelings of happiness and achievement.

Maybe the activities you enjoy are mostly solo pursuits like reading, creative writing, sewing, painting, or wood-working. Why not create a social media profile for your works and show them off? Follow similar pages and leave positive comments on their photos or share your posts among family or on local pages. You'll be reaching out to warm and encouraging communities from all over the world and interacting with a huge range of people who enjoy the same hobbies.

I Don't Feel Confident

Low confidence is one of the biggest obstacles to making friends. If you don't feel you can put yourself out there, no one is going to see you. Remember those puberty hormones that are slowly transforming you into an adult? Affecting your confidence is another one of their "fun" side effects. Having confidence in yourself means you are certain that you can do something, or will be able to with the right support. This confidence usually stems from good knowledge of your own abilities. When I had to hire a large van to move some furniture, I was confident I could drive it despite never having done so before, because I knew I could drive a car well and I trusted my ability to adapt to leaving more room at corners and finding a larger parking space.

But when you don't have confidence in yourself to behave appropriately in a social situation, it makes trying something new a million times harder. Maybe you don't trust your new, weird teenage body. You're worried you'll blush, or sweat, or say the wrong thing. Maybe you're worried you'll walk into the room and instantly faceplant because you've been extra clumsy lately. Not being able to trust your own body to do the right thing would be a huge blow to anyone's confidence.

One simple way to improve your self-confidence is to put yourself in a situation where you feel more in control. Like in the previous section, you can use your hobbies and passions to help you. If you're confident in your ability to play guitar, why not try out for a band, or advertise for people to join you and make a new one? Many great bands have formed this way, including R.E.M, Radiohead, and Green Day. Play a piece you've practiced well so you'll be sure you can do it to a good standard. The same goes for approaching sports teams; let your existing ability do the talking for you.

Other ways of boosting your confidence include meeting people in places you know well or having existing friends, family, or teachers nearby. Just having someone familiar and friendly in the same room, without them interacting with you, can be a huge boost to your confidence.

I'm going to go into more detail about how to improve your confidence in chapter six, including some ways you can use body language to appear more confident to others, even if you're still a nervous wreck inside.

Social Situations Make Me Anxious

This is something that many adults still struggle with today, including a few you wouldn't expect. Did you know that Adele struggles with anxiety attacks every time she performs? She's doing something she's good at, something that she's done thousands of times before, but that doesn't matter. You see, anxiety is a physical response that your body has to a stressful situation, and the more you're worried about something, the stronger the reaction is.

Here's what happens when you have to do something that makes you feel stressed. That could be having to read out something in class, take a test, or run away from a hungry bear. Whatever stresses you, your body does the same thing; it releases a stream of chemicals called adrenaline and cortisol. I mentioned them back in chapter one as the "stress hormones" because whenever you're stressed, they're sent in to help. You see, these stress hormones are supposed to help you deal with whatever problem you're facing by supercharging your body. They make your heart beat faster so it can send more blood to your brain or your muscles, depending on where it's needed. The idea is to help you perform better, so you read more confidently, focus better on the test questions, or run faster from Mr. Grizzly.

However, with the exception of grizzly bear attacks, most of the stresses you'll meet on a daily basis don't really need your body to be faster, stronger, or hyper focused. Instead, the increased heart rate can make you feel a little dizzy, and because your body is preparing to perform superhuman feats of speed or strength, it shuts down other functions that aren't needed, diverting power from one organ to another. So your mouth goes dry because you don't need saliva to fight a bear and you feel cold and clammy because warming your skin isn't as beneficial as warming your muscles.

These physical sensations of stress and anxiety can be extremely unpleasant, and if you know that doing something is going to make you feel like this, it's completely understandable that you'd want to avoid it. In chapter five, you'll find some exercises to help you get used to these feelings and minimize their effects, as well as some ways to stop feeling so stressed about social situations in general.

I'm New Here, and Everyone Else Is Already Friends

Being a transfer student, coming back from a long period of illness, or losing an existing group of friends can leave you feeling lonely. There's nothing worse than seeing everyone else in happy little groups because from where you're standing, those groups seem complete. The problem with this attitude is that no friendship group is ever complete. People do move in and out of them, as well as belong to more than one. Remember: Teenagers are biologically designed to seek out other like-minded people because they're like a wolf pack; there's safety in numbers.

If you put yourself in the places where you are happy and feel confident—the sports hall, the music block, or the library, for example—you will instantly be making yourself available to people with similar interests. If you see a group of teens doing something you enjoy, introduce yourself. Smile, be open and friendly, and give them a compliment or ask for their opinion or help with something related to their activity. Maybe it's a film or book recommendation, or some help learning a new trick, chord, or technique. Everyone responds well to praise and positivity; if you lead with it you give yourself the best chance of success.

There's Absolutely No One Like Me

Trying to find like-minded people can be all the more difficult if you already feel like an outcast. When you focus too much on what makes you different from the people around you, you risk missing everything that you have in common. This is such a common feeling; there are hundreds of teen novels and movies that set up the main character as an outcast. Maybe they moved from the city to the country, are in foster care, are LGBT+, or a minority race. Eventually they form an unlikely friendship with another student—or occasionally a vampire—bonding over the fact that they both like some obscure death metal band or can both recite pi to over a hundred places.

The point is, you *assume* there's no one like you, but until you have introduced yourself to everybody on the planet, you can never really know. It might take a bit more work on your part, but the chances are, if you like something, believe in something, or define yourself in some way, there are other people nearby who do too.

Chapter Four

What if People Don't Like Me?

IF YOU DON'T BELIEVE in yourself, why is anyone else going to believe in you? –Tom Brady

What if I Don't Like Me?

With all the changes going on during puberty, it's understandable that you might be finding it hard to love yourself. We've already talked about the physical changes you're going through, and there's nothing more frustrating than having a body that won't do or look the way you desperately want it to. You might be feeling extra clumsy because your body has suddenly grown and you aren't used to it yet. Or you might hate the fact that your face keeps breaking out in pimples. Increased testosterone also lowers your voice, but while your body adjusts, you'll have to put up with it squeaking occasionally. Increased estrogen causes breast tissue to grow and your hips to appear curvier. Both of these changes are very obvious to others, and it's easy to assume that everyone in the room is thinking about or judging how your body is changing. Some of them will be; that's unavoidable. But they're probably not as critical about things as you are.

When you were a kid it's likely that you didn't really think much about how the outside world saw you. If you wanted to wear a neon green tracksuit to the park, you did it. And if some horrible little brat told you it looked like you were wearing snot, you probably responded with "your face looks like snot" and ran off laughing. But now that your teenage brain is capable of imagining what others are thinking, you want to take a lot more care of how you look. Not only because you've started to care about looking good, but because you want to minimize the chances of negative comments from other people, especially if they're peers whose opinion you value.

The emotional changes of adolescence can also be upsetting to go through. No one enjoys being an unpredictable bag of emotions. You'll find yourself overreacting to something and wondering why you did that. Being out of your go-to snack can now be a meltdown-inducing trigger and you'll find yourself going from happy to distraught or furious in a matter of milliseconds. Bouncing around the entire spectrum of emotions in one day is exhausting, and that's without dealing with all the people who are upset and confused by your reactions.

How are you supposed to feel positively about yourself when you don't feel in control? Try and focus on the things that you do like about yourself, even if they seem small and insignificant compared to everything you wish you could change. Some people find it helpful to keep a small notebook or a jar filled with positive statements that they can look back through when they feel bad. It might sound silly, but reading nice things about yourself really does make you feel a little bit better. You could even get some friends or family members to add some-thing.

It's extremely likely that you will never like everything about yourself. So your nose is a little wonky; does that make you a horrible person? Does it condemn you to a life of solitude and misery? Absolutely not! Adolescence is hard enough without you putting yourself down. Learn to love—or at least tolerate—what makes you different.

It's All in Your Head

One of the main changes brought about by puberty is that you become self-conscious. That's often a term used to describe people who are aware of, and worry about, things about themselves that they view in the negative. In its simplest terms, it just means that you are aware that you exist as a person with a personality, feelings, emotions, and preferences. The problems occur when you remember that you're also now becoming aware of others and trying to work out where you fit into the world of high school and adolescence.

So many teenagers look at others around them and see things they would rather have or rather be, and that makes them think more negatively about themselves. If you walk into school and see someone showing off their new jacket, you might become more aware that yours is looking a little shabby. Then you might start to worry that people will notice this and either tease you for it or think badly of you. This can affect your self-esteem.

Self-esteem is slightly different to self-consciousness. Being overly self-conscious about your own qualities can negatively effect self-esteem. Your self-esteem is how you feel about yourself. So if you have high self-esteem, it means you feel generally positive about yourself and your life and you feel confident in your ability to handle situations. It's quite common for teenagers to suffer from low self-esteem where they feel that they aren't worthy of good things like friendship, good grades, and positive attention, and are going to fail because they aren't good enough.

Here's an example that shows how having high or low self-esteem can affect a simple interaction:

You're in a clothes store looking for a new pair of shoes as you have some birthday money to spend. There's a pair you really like that are on display but you can't find your size. A sales clerk is hovering nearby.

High self-esteem: You take the shoes over to the sales clerk and ask if they have your size in stock. The clerk goes back to check and brings you the shoes in the correct size. You try them on, but unfortunately they're a bit tight. You hand them back, say thank you, and go to look elsewhere.

Low self-esteem: You wonder why the clerk is watching you. Maybe they think you're going to steal the shoes. They do look a lot nicer than your current shoes. The clerk comes over and asks if you need any help. You weren't expecting that. Your mouth dries up and you can't think of what to say. You shake your head and leave the shop. You don't go to look in any others because you don't want to risk repeating the interaction.

In our second example, your low self-esteem made you feel unworthy of the nice shoes, and because you felt that way, you projected it onto other people. Projecting your own negative opinions onto others can make you feel as if everyone you meet automatically knows all the bad things about you (even though there probably aren't many).

Making Yourself More Appealing

I've already said that this book is not going to try and change who you are. But this is where we start to address some behaviors you have that might not be helping you to make friends as easily as you would like. Some of these are going to be pretty simple fixes, and others are going to need a lot of commitment and work from you. It's important to remember that you don't need to change everything at once. Pick something that you think you can easily work on; this will give you an almost immediate sense of satisfaction and encourage you to try another. A series of small successes will make you feel better about yourself, and that change in attitude will shine through and inspire others to view you more positively too.

Wash Your Troubles Away

Personal hygiene is never more important than during your teenage years, yet this is often something that adolescents fail to give due care to. You might have been able to get away with the occasional bath as a child, but now your sweat glands are working overtime—thanks again, puberty! You'll find that you sweat more, even if you don't do anything energetic. When sweat mixes with bacteria, it makes a strong, unpleasant smell. Delightful! Sweat and bacteria can build up if not washed away, and this makes the odor even stronger.

Teenagers can be quick to judge, and no one wants to be labeled as the smelly kid, because that nickname won't wash away, no matter how frequently you shower. Getting into a good personal hygiene routine will make you feel more confident because you will know that you look clean and smell fresh. So what are the basics you need to take care of?

- Take a shower every day. Wash with soap or shower gel and clean water and pay special attention to the places where sweat builds up. These include your armpits, feet, under breasts, and the top of your thighs; basically, anywhere where there are skin folds or where you wear tight-fitting clothing. Avoid using scented soaps on your genitals, as the perfumes in them can sometimes cause an allergic reaction.

- Wear deodorant or antiperspirant. These work in different ways and you might find one more effective than the other. Antiperspirants prevent you from sweating whereas deodorants just obscure the smell. If you find you sweat a lot, antiperspirants are probably the best for you. Both work best when applied to clean skin—just adding more over the top of already smelly pits doesn't help as much as you think it does!

- Change out of sweaty clothes. You should have different outfits for sports so you can change into something clean and fresh when you have finished. Once something has been worn, add it to the laundry pile; don't be tempted to try and wear it again. If the temperature is warm, you might find yourself sweating more and ending up with wet patches on your clothes. Feel free to change your top a couple of times throughout the day if you feel uncomfortable.

- Wash your face. Acne is caused by your skin producing too much oil, not because your face is dirty. This excess oil clogs up your pores, causing pimples. However, if bacteria on your skin gets trapped in these clogged pores, it can cause inflammation leading to raised and unsightly red spots called pustules and papules. (NHS Choices, n.d.) Keeping your face clean can reduce the appearance of these, so make sure you wash once a day with clean, warm water. You can use soap or a specialized cleansing product, but be aware that some can dry out your skin, which will then cause other problems. Using a light moisturizer can help combat this. Bonus fun acne fact: Whether or not you get acne is defined by your genes, so if your parents had bad acne, chances are you will too.

- Menstrual hygiene. Periods start during adolescence and bring with them a whole new care routine. Make sure you replace or empty your period products regularly, even if your flow is light. Wash with water, never with soap or shower gel, even if it contains all natural ingredients. For advice and help with choosing the right products for you when you feel you can't talk to your caregivers, you can speak to your school nurse, family doctor, or find a local sexual health clinic.

How to Look Inviting

In the previous chapter, I mentioned some bad advice for meeting people and one of them said "smile more." I'm going to contradict myself now and explain why you should do exactly that! Indulge me a little; it will make sense in the end.

Whether you realize it or not, you can tell a person a lot about yourself without saying a word. Body language is a strange form of communication, because even if you're bad at reading it, you're still speaking it. Sometimes the messages that you're giving off are scaring people away, even if you don't mean to. I'll use my friend as an example. She never knows what to do with her hands, so if she isn't using them, she'll generally do one of two things: fold her arms across her chest or put her hands on her hips. The crossed arms give out mixed signals and can sometimes be read by other people as her saying "don't come here, or else" and the arms akimbo pose is aggressive and defiant. Both those signals are saying something she doesn't intend because all she's doing is trying not to fidget with her hands, which is something she does when nervous.

Wherever you are, you're continuously sending out and receiving signals like these. The gestures you make, your posture, your tone of voice, eye movements and how much eye contact you actually make... these are all being read by the people around you. Use the right body language cues and you can put people at ease, but send the wrong ones and you'll only confuse or offend them. The good intentions behind the advice to smile more are to get you to think about how you can make your body language more inviting.

- Smile. It's a universally recognised symbol for putting people at ease and signaling that everything is okay. You don't need to walk around with a fake grin permanently tattooed on your face; instead your smile should be given out when making eye contact with someone to indicate that you're not threatening them, but in fact, inviting further interaction. It's specially effective if someone smiles at you first, because sending a smile back is like returning a serve on the tennis court.

- Avoid hoods, hats, and helmets. You don't want to hide your face; it makes people think that you're untrustworthy because you won't look them in the eye. Eye contact is a really important way that we communicate because our eyes themselves are very expressive.

- Don't hunch over. Open body language signals to others that it's okay to approach you. This means standing straight, not crossing your arms, and keeping your head up. Slouching and looking at the floor shows other people that you want to avoid them and tells them that they should probably keep clear. Not the messages you want to send out if you're trying to meet new people.

Unfortunately, a lot of the body language mentioned above is your default setting if you're nervous or uncomfortable and overriding that can take a lot of practice. Start with one thing, like setting a task to smile at three random people each day. After a while, you'll feel more at ease and the smile will feel more natural. It's a wonderful feeling when someone smiles back at you and, who knows, that might even spark a new friendship.

Be Where the People Are

I've already mentioned in the previous chapter about different ways you can try to connect with people who enjoy the same hobbies and interests as you. Some of them relied on you being proactive, but I'm aware that that isn't something everyone feels comfortable doing. Ideally, you would go somewhere and instantly be welcomed by a group of people, and that isn't an entirely impossible scenario. Getting yourself to as many different places as possible also makes it a lot easier for others to find you, and if you're there at the same time every week, you're more likely to meet the same people.

If the idea of committing to a regular club or starting a new course isn't something you can handle right now, then start small. Find a local spot—a park, the library, a cafe, even a particular bus route—and keep going there at the same time. You'll become a familiar face to the other people who are also there at that time and familiar things are comforting because they are reliable. I take my dog to the dog park at the same time every day and I see the same people there because it's as much a part of their routine as it is mine. I know all the dogs' names but very few of their owners', but that doesn't matter because we still chat about the weather, last night's sports, or the current political dramas. If something happens and I have to go later, a new set of people are there and the park suddenly feels a lot less friendly. No one knows me, so no one comes over to chat. You need to find your own version of the dog park and make yourself a part of it. Then practice some of that positive body language you've just read about.

If you do feel ready to commit to something more involving but can't find a local club for an existing hobby, you could always take the plunge and try something new. Why not see what is available to you and do a bit of online research to see what it would be like? Watch some YouTube videos of some of the sports or exercise classes offered at the sports hall. You never know what you'll find interesting; you might be looking for a ballet class and end up taking dancersize instead!

What's the Worst That Can Happen?

In all likelihood, there are some of you who read all those suggestions and felt nothing but panic. It's easy for me to put those ideas on the page, but another thing completely for the person who has to try them out. Remember: Start small. Maybe all you can manage this week is an internet search for local clubs and picking five that you want to look at again. That's great progress! Every step forward, no matter how small, is still moving in the right direction.

A lot of the time, what stops you from doing something, is the idea that it will go wrong or horrible things will happen. It all links back to your developing brain and its tendency to over analyze every new situation. Once you start to imagine negative experiences, your body takes over by releasing hormones to deal with this stressful situation, even though it is only hypothetical. Well, two can play at that game.

If your body is going to set off a stress reaction because of something you only thought about, you can also use your thoughts to work through the things you are worried about and show your brain that actually, the worst probably won't happen. These techniques make use of a few fundamental elements of cognitive behavioral therapy (CBT). CBT aims to help people make changes to the way they behave by changing the way they think about different situations. (Walker, 2021). It does this through a series of exercises to help people analyze where their negative thoughts come from and to learn to use this process to make changes to their behavior.

Drilling to the Core of the

Problem

People are notoriously bad at analyzing their own thoughts and actions. Have you ever struggled to check your schoolwork and find any mistakes but passed it to a partner and they found some? It's because when we've made a mistake once, we tend to make it again, and when we're looking over our own work or our own actions, we tend to gloss over the bad parts.

This next exercise is going to help you analyze why you find something difficult. Once you know what the core problem is, you can work specifically on treating that issue. It's the difference between a doctor treating a symptom or the disease. For example, you have a bacterial chest infection, which is giving you a cough and a fever. Treating the symptoms—cough and fever—will make you feel better for a bit, but they will come back again. Taking antibiotics will get rid of the infection for good, and that will also get rid of the cough and fever.

Let's look at one of our common problems from earlier: Social situations make me anxious. It's easy to assume that the anxiety comes from being in a room with other people, but I bet there's a deeper cause. Otherwise, you'd find it impossible to be anywhere with anyone. I'm going to give you an example of how you can use something called the downward arrow technique to probe deeper into your real feelings about a situation.

The downward arrow technique is a series of questions, each one adding more detail to the previous answer. It's a bit like ordering a drink at Starbucks.

"Can I have a hot chocolate please?"

"Sure. Would you like a syrup in that?"

"Caramel, please."

"And would you like whipped cream and marshmallows?"

"Ooh that sounds great, yes please."

"Would you like oat milk, 2%, 1%, or fat-free?"

"Fat-free, thanks."

"Are you having it here or to go?"

You get the idea. We've gone from a generic drink to a very specific order that is unique to you. Similarly, we're going to do the same with the anxiety. Lots of teens suffer from anxiety in social situations, but they all have different reasons for it.

Downward Arrows in Practice

To start working through your downward arrows technique, you first need to hone in on a specific situation that makes you uncomfortable. In my example, I'm going to use a common scenario you might find yourself in at school:

I have to eat my lunch in the lunch hall, which is full of people I don't know.

You probably have some avoidance techniques you put into practice to minimize the stress you feel at lunch time. These might include:

- choosing a table close to the door so you can eat quickly and leave

- skipping lunch

- taking a book or some homework to do while you eat

- putting headphones on

In this scenario, you're going to imagine what will happen if you don't do any of your usual avoidance behaviors. Keep asking yourself what will happen, even if you feel you're caught in a loop, until you find the big worry at the core.

Here's how your questions might go:

What will happen?

Someone might come and sit next to me and they'll start talking to me.

What will happen if someone sits next to you and talks to you?

I'll feel really nervous and won't know what to say. My mouth will get dry and I might say something stupid.

What will happen if you feel nervous and say something stupid?

They'll look at me like I'm a weirdo. I'll feel so embarrassed, I'll probably turn bright red.

What will happen if you feel embarrassed and turn red?

I'll either clam up completely or start babbling because I'll be trying to divert their attention from my face. Either way, they'll definitely start making fun of me.

What will happen if they make fun of you?

Everyone else will start making fun of me too.

What will happen if everyone makes fun of you?

It won't just be the lunch hall where I'll feel uncomfortable, it will be everywhere at school.

What will happen if you feel uncomfortable at school?

I'll start feeling ill every day I go and might start skiving. I won't be able to concentrate in class and my grades will slip.

As you can see, at each step of the questioning, I've tried to concentrate on what you think will happen and how it will make you feel. We've looked at what the main reason for avoiding the lunch hall is—being worried that some-one will talk to you and you'll embarrass yourself—to the deeper reason behind why that is such a problem:

It will be so horrible that it will completely affect your performance in school.

Creating Your Own World

Now that we know the problem is not knowing what will happen when someone talks to you, we can move on to the next exercise. This is a simple visualization technique, which can be used when the thought of changing something in a real setting is too difficult, scary, or dangerous. Now, talking to other teenagers over a sandwich is hardly dangerous; it's not like they're going to stab you with a tortilla chip and pelt you with luncheon meat. But visualization is a good way of taking a smaller step forward when a big one seems unmanageable.

Here's how it works: You're going to imagine yourself in the scenario you're struggling with. So, in this example, you imagine yourself in the lunch hall with none of your avoidance behavior or minimizing apparatus. Make the imagined visit as real as possible, as if you were controlling a dream. You're going to start picturing yourself walking down the corridor to the lunch hall. Do you have to open the doors? Remember to think about how you're feeling at this point.

Imagine you sit down in a seat you have chosen before. Look around you and fill in the rest of the room. Picture the other pupils and try to remember the sounds and smells that are also there. In your head, sit there and eat your lunch. Watch people fill up the other seats near you but leave your own table empty, for now. When you've finished your lunch, imagine yourself packing up and leaving the room.

The whole visualization will probably last about 5–10 minutes. It's important that you aren't disturbed while you do this, so make sure you're somewhere private and quiet. In order to be fully immersed in your thoughts, you'll need to make sure there are no outside lights or noises. If it's always loud at home, try wearing head-phones (without playing music) or pulling a hat over your ears to try and block some of the sounds.

While you're working through your imagined scenario, you should notice your stress levels beginning to rise, just like they would in real life. But because you are in control, you know that nothing bad is going to happen. Run the whole scenario again over the next few days and the parts that made you feel anxious will not seem too scary anymore. Our bodies are conditioned to react to certain stimuli. If you see a ball flying at you, you'll duck. If you see a tack on your chair, you won't sit down. If you walk into that lunch hall, you'll feel nervous. Because if your body doesn't react that way, something bad could happen. By imagining the same situation but without the negative association, you're taking the first steps to retrain your brain and your body.

Once you feel comfortable imagining the simple scenario, you can take it to the next level and keep increasing the difficulty over successive days. Here's how that progression might look for our example:

- Imagine other people sitting down at your table, but they don't talk to you.

- Imagine a specific person, who you find non-threatening, sits down next to you. They say hi and you say hi, then you eat your lunch in silence.

- Imagine you and that person have a simple conversation about something that happened in class.

- Imagine walking into the lunch hall and your usual seat is taken. The only seat is next to a group of other teenagers. You sit there instead. They acknowledge you as you sit down but don't try to talk to you.

- Imagine the above scenario, except they ask you some questions. Maybe they are arguing about whether physics or geography is more boring and want to know your opinion.

- Imagine walking into the lunch hall and having a few options of where to sit. When you sit down, say hi to the people at the table and then start the conversation yourself.

You can increase the stress levels of your own scenario at whatever speed you feel comfortable with. Some of you would need to take all the above steps and run through each visualization a number of times. Others might be able to jump straight to the conversations.

Remember the result of our downward arrow questions? We discovered that, in this scenario, the real reason the lunch hall was so scary was that someone could make fun of you, which would be so embarrassing your schoolwork would suffer. In none of the visualizations, does anything like this happen. That's a whole lot of positive reinforcement for your brain.

Chapter Five

Why do I Have to Leave My Comfort Zone?

*S*OME PEOPLE WANT IT *to happen, some wish it would happen, others make it happen.* –Michael Jordan

Some Boundaries Are Good... and Some Aren't

We love boundaries because they make us feel safe. From fences at the zoo that separate us from the lions and tigers, to laws that deter people from driving recklessly; boundaries are everywhere. When you were a small child, your caregivers were in charge of setting your limits and making sure you knew what you could and couldn't do. As an adult, you have more control over deciding your own—as long as you also obey those set by society.

Adolescence is all about repositioning those boundaries. Sometimes you'll have complete free reign to decide where you want to move them to, other times it will require negotiation with the adults around you. Other times it will seem like all-out war! But even though there are many boundaries you're actively pushing against, you will also find some you aren't ready to move, even if others are pressuring you to make a change.

Everyone has their own comfort zone. It's not a physical location, rather a collection of things you feel entirely comfortable doing. Inside your comfort zone, you are in control, more productive, and achieve better results. When we are doing something that is within our comfort zone, we usually feel happy and don't experience any stress or anxiety. By contrast, having to do something that you consider to be outside of your comfort zone often immediately raises your heart rate, causes you to sweat, and makes your stomach do that weird flippy thing like you're on a rollercoaster.

What can make you anxious about leaving your comfort zone? We've already looked at how past negative experiences can impact how you feel about trying something in the future. Maybe you once spoke up in class and your comments completely fell flat. You worry that if you do it again, you'll get the same response, so you now avoid answering questions or offering ideas. It's a completely understandable reaction. Some people don't even need a previous bad experience to convince themselves that nothing good will happen. Just imagining the whole class laughing because you got the answer wrong would be enough to keep your hand firmly down during class.

Time to Break Out

If just thinking about leaving your comfort zone is so horrible, why bother doing it at all? For most people, our comfort zones include a wide array of skills, activities, locations, and people. There is enough there to happily sustain us throughout our lives. It used to be assumed that you had to leave your comfort zone in order to learn anything new, but it's now more widely accepted that your comfort zone itself is the perfect environment within which to nurture and develop new skills. For example, if you love writing poetry but want to try writing short stories, that is a new skill that would still be within your comfort zone. However, if you wanted to go to a slam poetry night and read your creations to a crowd, that might be outside your comfort zone, and the experience could be stressful.

Problems arise when your comfort zone is unmanageably small. For many reasons, there are people who go through life never really feeling comfortable with anything. If your comfort zone is limited to playing video games in your bedroom and anything else makes you feel extremely anxious, you are obviously going to have problems when life starts demanding more from you. Living your life in a constant state of anxiety and stress isn't just bad for your mental health; your physical health will suffer too. Spending too long feeling stressed can lead to headaches, difficulty sleeping, weight problems, and high blood pressure.

Stepping outside of your comfort zone on your own terms should produce less anxiety than being thrust out of it by evil forces beyond your control. For example, if talking to strangers is outside of your comfort zone, you could work on your anxiety by using visualization exercises and building yourself up to saying hi to people in the school corridors or in a store.

Outside the Comfort Zone

Obviously, we can't all live in our imagination forever. While visualizations are an excellent technique to start overcoming your anxieties, at some point you're going to have to test yourself with some real-world exposures. This is where you intentionally expose yourself to a stressful situation in order to continue conditioning your brain that the worst stuff it can imagine really isn't going to happen. Because you are going to plan and design your own exposure experiences, you will retain a lot of control over the situation, but not as much as you did if you were conducting a visualization.

Real-world exposures need a bit more planning than imagined ones. You want to make sure that you consider as many factors that could affect the situation as possible so that nothing comes as a surprise. You also want to make sure you can repeat your exposure every day—or at least for the days you are in school—as this is how it will be most effective.

Plan the Least Uncomfortable Discomfort

So, what do you need to consider when planning your exposure experience? Obviously, that will depend on what your particular situation is, but you need to consider factors that will increase or decrease the stress factors for you. Thinking about our lunch hall example, these could include the following:

- What time do you visit the lunch hall? Does the school have staggered meal times for different year groups? Does everyone rush there at the start of lunch, meaning it will be emptier if you wait a bit?

- Is one day of the week typically busier than others? Maybe because of the different food on offer?

- Are there any clubs that affect how many and what type of people are there? Going at the same time as football practice would mean fewer jocks in the hall, whereas going at the same time as debate club or a theater trip would reduce the number of other types of students.

- Do you have a lunch time club or arrangement that you have to go to after you've eaten? It's best not to rush your experience, as you will be feeling the pressure to eat and leave quickly.

- What lesson do you have directly before lunch? This will affect how you feel going into lunch and whether you are already stressed. What about after lunch? Would you be extra anxious if running your exposure experience might affect it?

Look back through your answers, use them to identify the least stressful time for your first exposure. You don't need to tell anyone what you're planning to do, but you might find it useful to confide in a friend or a trusted adult, so that they can help you process it afterward. You might find it useful to talk through anything that happened that you weren't expecting, or you might just want to tell someone that you successfully battled an inner demon. You could also find it useful to keep a journal of your attempts and the thoughts you have about them. It will help you to look back over all the hard work you've put in and see how far you've come.

Emotions Versus Feelings

This seems like an appropriate time to discuss the difference between emotions and feelings. Quite often they're talked about like they're the same thing, but there are some pretty big differences. Emotions are your unconscious reactions to specific triggers, whereas feelings are the sensations in your body in response to an emotion or other outside effect. You can feel cold, tired, and hungry—these are not emotions or linked to emotions. You can also feel joyful, content, amused, and delighted; these are all responses to the emotion of being happy, and each one is distinct from the other.

The American Psychological Association describes anxiety as an emotion "characterized by feelings of tension, worried thoughts, and physical changes like increased blood pressure" (American Psychological Association, 2022). Within that description, you can see the feelings associated with anxiety: worry, stress, dizziness, disorientation, and light-headedness, which can be caused by raised blood pressure.

The reason I'm talking about feelings and emotions is that often the physical sensations caused by the feelings can be more unpleasant than experiencing the emotion itself. With anxiety, you probably find yourself feeling jittery, sweaty, and light-headed, and experience breathing difficulties, a dry mouth, a raised heart rate, and even chest pains. All those sensations are unpleasant, and the thought of going through that feeling contributes to the desire to avoid a situation. You're already worried that you'll do something embarrassing; now you're also worried you'll blush or start sweating. That makes you worry even more, see how it's all stacking up?

Just like you can use visualizations to prepare you for facing your anxieties in real life, you can also practice experiencing these uncomfortable feelings. Whatever sensation you find the most off-putting, there will be a way to artificially trigger it. For example, if you hate the feeling of blushing, you could try quickly drinking something hot or eating a big mouthful of something very spicy. This will trigger a flushed feeling in your face, chest, and the palms of your hands. The more times you can practice this, the more you will be able to tolerate the unpleasant feelings. Here are some other triggers:

- To induce sweating and breathlessness, do rapid exercise on the spot, similar to a HIIT workout. This could be running, jumping jacks, press ups, or even frenetic dancing!

- To simulate feeling shaky and weak, try holding a can of beans (or similar) in your outstretched arms for as long as you can manage. When you put them down your arms will feel like they do during a stressful moment when your body reroutes blood to the heart and brain. You can do the same to your legs by doing squats or holding the yoga position called chair pose.

- If you find yourself hyperventilating when anxious, you can practice intentional hyperventilation to get used to the feeling of light-headedness and difficulty breathing. This is safe for most people, but if you have asthma, heart problems, or suffer from seizures, it's best to give this exercise a miss. To intentionally hyperventilate, you should breathe in as deeply and as hard as you can, and then exhale just as forcefully. Repeat for about 20 seconds and then resume normal breathing.

When practicing any of these, make sure you then focus on how your body feels afterward. Make a mental note of how anxious that makes you feel. How does it compare to when you experience these sensations naturally? After a few repetitions, you should start to feel less anxious. This means that when you come across a stressful situation that triggers these feelings, that fact in itself won't contribute as strongly to your anxiety as it did before.

Into the Great Unknown

Now that you've analyzed your triggering situation and decided on the least scary way forward, what next? There's nothing left but to go for it. Make sure you prepare everything you need the night before, but don't be tempted to fall back on any of your usual comfort blankets. It's really important that you don't take anything with you that you would usually rely upon to help you avoid what is causing you anxiety. If you know it's there, you will find an excuse to use it.

If you need to, plan what route you are taking and make sure you leave in plenty of time so you are not rushed. Pack your bag or organize your locker in advance so you know you have every book, project, and piece of stationary you need. I'm going to give you a final example of how our lunch hall-avoiding student could carry out their exposure experience, and then I'll include an extra story running through all the exercises from start to finish so you've got another example to help you on your journey.

Exposure Example

You decide to run the first exposure experience on a Wednesday lunch hour. You have your best lesson beforehand and study hall afterward, so you're going to be less worried about how a stressful lunch time will impact the rest of the day. You've left a book and your headphones in your locker—you won't take them into the lunch hall but will need them for study hall if you are too upset to work. Wednesday is also basketball and lacrosse practice, so it's the emptiest day and that makes it more likely that you can get a seat of your choice. You've packed a simple sandwich that you know you can eat quickly and if you start to feel sick with anxiety, it won't make you sick.

You've decided that you'll sit on your own as close to the doors. If that isn't possible you have thought through a backup plan and will sit in any seat that has a space next to it. You're in luck though, there is a table near the door with one other person sitting at the end. They don't look up when you sit down, which makes you feel relieved. You take out your lunch and force yourself to eat the sandwich slowly. The other student leaves not long after and you relax a little.

You're nearly done when a group of younger students approaches your table. They're chatting loudly about their weekend plans. You feel your heart rate increase and you start to breathe quickly. They sit down but don't look around. You take the last two bites of your sandwich and leave the table. Your heart is pounding and you can hear the blood rushing through your ears. But it doesn't feel like the usual nerves this time; it feels more exciting. You realize it is because you made it through your exposure and nothing bad happened, even though other teens were sitting at your table. They didn't seem interested in talking to you—one of your main worries—which has made you feel more positive about doing it again on Thursday.

Alex's Story

Alex and Dan were best friends since the start of elementary school, but that all changed in eighth grade when Dan made the basketball team. Suddenly, Alex didn't have anyone to sit with at lunch anymore because Dan was always at practice. Then Dan stopped wanting to do anything after school because he was hanging out with his teammates instead.

Alex has a few other kids in his class who he doesn't mind talking to, but they don't invite him to anything outside of school. He feels abandoned by Dan and that makes him sad, so he is quieter than normal in class.

One day, the teacher asks him a question and Alex mumbles the answer. The teacher has to ask him to speak up, but he freezes. Some of the kids in his class laugh, which makes Alex withdraw even more. By the time school breaks up for the summer, his attendance has slipped because he makes himself sick to avoid going to school.

The thought of starting school again and not having any friends there is making Alex feel anxious. There are a few weeks to go before Alex starts high school and he doesn't want to start the year the same way it finished. Having had some time away from school has been good and he has enjoyed taking his younger brother camping and helping to teach him to play the drums. It made him realize that people do enjoy his company and has given him hope that he will make friends at his new school. But Alex knows he has some work to do first.

Alex wants to find a way to stop feeling anxious when he's around new people. He begins by practicing some breathing exercises because when he feels anxious, he starts to hyperventilate. By learning to calm himself down, Alex has a tool he can use at school when things get really bad. He can sit in the toilets and use a few minutes of deep breathing to slow his heart rate and get his breath back.

Alex also finds that when he gets anxious his mouth dries up and this feeling makes him gag. He then worries about throwing up in public and that makes the feelings of anxiety worse. Alex decides that if he gets used to the feeling of a dry mouth it won't make him feel sick anymore, and then he will have one less thing to worry about. He makes sure he has a glass of water ready and then uses a hairdryer to artificially dry out his mouth. The first few times he feels awful and gulps the water straight away, but after a few weeks he realizes it isn't making him feel sick anymore.

There will be lots of kids from his middle school going to the same high school, but there will be even more who are new. Alex worries that everyone will pick their new friends in the first few weeks and he will be left out again. An online friend suggests he use the downward arrows technique to help him better understand. This is what Alex draws:

My main worry: I won't make a friend in the first week.

What happens if you don't make a friend in the first week?

Everyone else will have someone to talk to except me.

What happens if everyone has someone to talk to except you?

I'll feel lonely.

What happens if you feel lonely?

I'll withdraw again.

What happens if you withdraw?

They'll all think there's something wrong with me. There must be if no one wants to be my friend.

What happens if they think there's something wrong with you?

They'll start picking on me, and we're older now, so it'll be worse.

What happens if they start picking on you?

I'll withdraw even more. Last time, the thought of going to school made me sick and I used it as an excuse to stay at home.

What happens if you miss school?

I'll miss out on everything and no one will fill me in because they won't even notice I'm not there.

Alex realizes that he is most worried about missing out on the fun things about being a teenager, because he doesn't have anyone to share them with. He knows there are some things he can do by himself, like join some clubs. This will give him more of a chance to meet people with the same interests as him. He decides that he had a lot of fun camping in the summer, so he looks up his local Scout group and sends them an email. It makes him feel good that he has taken a step toward doing something social. He starts to feel excited rather than anxious.

In the week before high school starts, Alex decides to give himself an extra confidence boost by doing some visualization exercises. He imagines himself walking into his new classroom on the first day and finding an empty seat. He tries a couple of different scenarios and decides he is less anxious when he imagines choosing a seat after most of the class has already sat down. When he imagines himself being first into the classroom, he starts to worry that people will choose not to sit near him. He knows if he arrives on time, he will have a few seats to choose from, so he sets his alarm 10 minutes earlier to make sure he isn't late.

Alex also imagines himself making small talk with someone he sits near. He keeps the conversation simple by asking the other person what they did over the summer. He makes sure to use open and friendly body language so they know he is listening, and then he asks follow-up questions. He practices smiling in the mirror and sitting with his shoulders back so he looks more relaxed.

The day before school, Alex gets an email back from the Scouts inviting him to their next meeting. This gives him a boost of positivity and something to look forward to in case school doesn't go well. He packs his bag, makes sure he knows the route to walk, and tries to get an early night's sleep.

Alex has done everything he can to give himself the best chance of battling his anxieties and getting to know new people at school. He felt more confident because he had practiced his visualizations beforehand and planned how he would attempt his first exposure. He may not make a friend on the first day, but he will start making connections that could turn into deeper friendships, both at school and at the Scouts.

Chapter Six

Fake It Until You Make It!

*D*ON'T BE AFRAID OF *failure. This is the way to succeed.*
–LeBron James

One unexpected thing that happens to your brain is that it manages to convince you that you can now read minds. You know that feeling when you walk into a room, everyone turns to look at you, and straight away you know they're all thinking the same thing? Yeah, I'm sorry to break it to you, but you can't actually tell what they're all thinking. You think they're all staring at that massive pimple on your chin, but most of them probably haven't even noticed it. They're looking at you because you walked into the room and created a distraction from whatever else they were concentrating on, or avoiding concentrating on.

Even better, did you know that none of them are mind readers either? So, you might think that they can all tell that you're late to class because you were in the bathroom suffering the after effects of "meatball Monday" in the lunch hall, but there's no way they can actually possibly know that.

A lot of teenage anxieties are linked to what you think other people are thinking. You can't help it; it's a new upgrade for your brain and you're still trying to get a grip on it. If you spend all your time wondering what other people are going to think of you before you do something, you're going to be stressed and exhausted. There's no way you can predict what everyone else is going to think or do all of the time.

This is why we seek to surround ourselves with friends. They are predictable, so we can spend less time trying to second-guess their actions, and they like us, so their opinions and comments are going to be largely positive. But friends don't magically appear—if they did then you wouldn't be reading this book—and if you think you're the only person without them, that can be a pretty lonely feeling.

It feels like a particularly cruel trick of nature that teens become convinced that everyone else is better, happier, more successful, or more attractive than them at a point in their lives when they need each other most. You're feeling alienated from your caregivers because they don't understand you and alienated from your peers because you're convinced they've got their shit together when you feel like you're falling apart. And how can they not? Look at all those other teenagers, happily chatting away to the lab partner they only met two minutes ago, while you grin awkwardly at yours and they look at you like they're staring at an idiot.

Behind the Curtain

I'm here to let you in on their dirty little secret: They're all thinking the same thing about you. Yes, there will be people in your class who think it's you who is better and happier than them. They admire that you don't feel the need to ingratiate yourself to everyone, that you have the self-confidence to proudly show off your own likes and dislikes, rather than trying to copy everyone else. They're babbling away to their lab partner hoping they sound halfway competent, wishing they didn't feel the need to be such a people pleaser all the time.

You may not believe it, but it's true. Remember, adolescence is the great equalizer: You and your peers are all going to go through the same experience of puberty, regardless of your race, background, social standing, or how rich your family are. Puberty doesn't care how many parents you have, how many schools you've attended, where you live, or how you identify. It's coming for you regardless. What makes this experience appear different from the outside, however, *is* shaped by your life experiences so far.

Teenagers who find socializing easy and aren't immediately reduced to a panicking mess in new social situations have already developed the confidence they need to deal with everything being thrown at them during that particular moment in time. They might also be the same person who bursts into tears if they miss the bus because they don't know how to make alternative arrangements, or they might fall to pieces the first time they get a failing grade in their best subject. Similarly, there are things you will do without batting an eyelid that they would need a book to guide them through.

Here's another secret: Because no one else can read your mind, they won't be able to tell what you're thinking. That sounds obvious, but at a time when you are biologically predisposed to worry about what everyone else thinks of you, everyone is busy trying to analyze each other's behaviors. You assume that you're getting it right, but we've already seen how damaging this assumption can be. Take the following example:

You are assigned Luke as a partner in Phys. Ed. You've never spoken to him before, but you happen to be standing near each other, so the coach pairs you up. You glance up at him and note that he looks more athletic than you. You also note that he doesn't smile. Great. He's annoyed to be paired with someone he thinks probably can't catch a ball.

What assumptions were made in that split second?

- Luke is better at sports than you.

- Luke is unhappy to be paired with you.

- You won't be as good as him.

- Luke knows all this, and it's why he doesn't want to work with you.

To your developing adolescent brain, it's all so obvious. You don't think you're good at sports, so everyone else must think the same. If you don't have any confidence in yourself, why would anyone else have confidence in you? But if you read that paragraph through again, you might notice that Luke does absolutely nothing to let you know what he's thinking. The absence of a smile is not a reliable indicator of his disapproval.

Confidence Breeds Confidence

If a lack of confidence is what's leading you to project your insecurities onto others, then what can you do about it? You can't magically make yourself more confident, no matter how many magic lamps you buy on the internet. What you can do is learn to give off the appearance of confidence. This will have two different effects: You will spend less time worrying what people think about you because you know they think you are confident, and second, after a while, that disguise of confidence will be replaced by the real thing.

Why is it important to appear confident even if you don't feel it on the inside? We are drawn to people who look confident because they seem to be in charge and in control of any situation. Who do you look to if there is an emergency; for example, if there was a fire in school? It would be those people who are confidently giving out instructions and leading people toward the exits. Would you feel as safe if the person trying to take charge was stammering the directions while wringing their hands and staring at their feet? Probably not.

We've already touched briefly on how you can unconsciously be giving off the wrong body language. Luckily these messages can be overwritten by consciously reprogramming yourself to give off more positive messages instead.

Teaching Your Body to Speak Confidently

One of the easiest ways to look confident is to increase the space you take up. Normally, when you don't feel confident about something, you try to shrink away from it. This can look like slouching, stooping, folding arms or putting hands in pockets, standing with legs together, or leaning away while sitting down. Have you ever found yourself feeling uncomfortable and trying to hide away in a corner of the room? All the signals you're giving out say "leave me alone," and they're throwbacks from the animal kingdom when prey would try to hide from predators.

Instead, when you're interacting with someone, make a concerted effort to stand up straight. Keep your hands out of your pockets and make eye contact with whoever you're talking to. Not in a creepy way—please, remember to blink! This presents a far more welcoming image and will set the other person at ease. Why? Because a lot of body language interpretation is down to context. We're not wild animals anymore, which means we don't need to be afraid of predators. So when you send out the signals that you would rather be anywhere else than talking to the person you're with, their vulnerable teenage brain is going to take that to mean there's something about them you want to avoid. Assuming that they overreact to things as much as you do, they will then start to wonder if they have spinach in their teeth, pronounced a word wrong, or are just so pathetic that it hurts you to speak to them.

I've already mentioned smiling as a great way to appear more inviting, and this works particularly well when combined with eye contact. Once again, it adds context to the nonverbal communication and lets whoever you're looking at know that you are friendly and approachable. Eye contact without a smile can be unnerving and make someone feel uncomfortable.

Nonverbal communication isn't just about body language, it also includes the way that we say something. Teenagers are notorious for snapping, shouting, and sounding sarcastic and these are all off-putting tones. If you want to engage in a conversation with someone, you should keep your tone of voice as friendly as possible and try not to make jokes or sarcastic comments that they might not understand. Also, think about the volume you're speaking at. If you're too quiet, then people won't hear you, but if you raise your voice too much, you could seem aggressive and overbearing. To appear more confident, make sure you're speaking clearly, which means at a reasonable volume and not too quickly. Unconfident people mumble quietly, hoping that no one will hear them so they won't be able to make fun of anything they've said.

What you do when you're not speaking is important too. When you are talking to someone else or a group of others, make sure you listen to their side of the conversation too. When you're trying to think of what to say, how you're saying it, and are also trying to make sure you're standing up straight and not staring intently ahead, it can be really easy to zone out while the other people are talking. But paying attention and responding to others is important in making them feel valued. It will also help you keep the flow of the conversation going because they will give you something to respond to. A conversation is a back and forth between two people and it simply doesn't work if one person does all the talking or keeps all the focus on them.

If all these tips sound daunting, don't worry. I don't expect you to master them all overnight. A lot of them can be practiced in front of a mirror, or you could record yourself on your smartphone or laptop and watch it back to see if you can spot examples of when you exhibit positive or negative body language. Choose one or two to start with and spend a few minutes each day switching between your natural body language and what you are trying to learn. Why not watch a movie and see if you can spot the nonverbal communication used by the actors? For example, one of the Marvel movies will show you a lot of confident body language from the superheroes and give you an idea of how it's supposed to look. Or a lot of high school dramas include a shy character who eventually finds their place, and you can see how their body language changes as the film goes on.

Learn to Mirror

A quick way to fake your confidence is to engage in a technique called "mirroring." This is often used by detectives—including yours truly—to quickly build a rapport with interview subjects and put them at ease, and it can work just as well for forming friendships with your peers. It's based on body language that happens naturally between friends and if someone is mirroring you, it's a strong indicator that they're interested in what you're saying.

What is mirroring? There's a not-so-subtle clue in the name. Basically, it means copying—mirroring—the body language of someone you're focused on. If you've ever watched one of those reality shows where people are coupled up for your entertainment, body language experts will often comment when two of them are mirroring each other's movements and declare it to be a sign that they're falling truly, madly, deeply in love for real. That's how strong a connection can be formed by mirroring movements. It shows that you're comfortable in each other's company and are enjoying spending time together.

You might be wondering if it's ethical to fake something that typically indicates a deep connection. If you're going to use the relationship for devious purposes—like some con men do when they lead people on romantically or convince them to hand over large amounts of cash—then yes, that would make you a bit of an asshole. But when you're making a genuine attempt to create a friendship, then this is something that you would be doing naturally, if it wasn't for anxiety and low self-esteem getting in the way.

So, how do you mirror someone without making it obvious? It works best if you're sitting or standing opposite each other. Look at the way they have positioned themselves. Is one foot further forward than the other or are their legs crossed? Do they use their hands a lot while talking or are they folded or placed on their knees? You want to subtly mirror their stance, so if their left leg is forward, you would put your right leg forward.

Also, look out for movements and actions they perform that you can copy, although don't do it instantly. For example, if they have a habit of tucking their hair behind their ears, you would perform the same movement on the opposite side. If they shift position, maybe crossing their legs the opposite way or switching which hand is in their pockets, you can wait a minute and then do the same.

Having your body language mirrored makes you feel relaxed, so not only will you be helping to lay the foundations for a good relationship with someone new, you will also be helping them feel at ease. Because remember, no matter how confident someone looks on the surface, you never know what insecurities they're hiding underneath.

The Ultimate Disguise

One thing that many teenagers continue to worry about is that their peers will see right through their attempts to appear more confident, or that they'll somehow know straight away that they are trying an exposure. Remember, puberty doesn't make anyone into a psychic. It's highly unlikely that anyone will even notice you are trying something different, let alone call you out on it. Trying something new, whether that's a hobby or believing in yourself, can feel scary and intimidating, but that isn't a reason not to do it.

Knowing that a lot of your insecurities about other people's opinions are down to the fact that your brain is behaving irrationally might help you feel more confident about making some small changes. As always, you should move at a speed that you feel you can handle. For some of you, that will be walking into school on Monday and making eye contact with five people in the corridors. For others, it will involve striking up entire conversations. Or it might be that you don't look at your feet when you give your ticket to the bus driver. Every step forward, no matter how small, is movement in the right direction. And, if you stride confidently into the classroom and someone points at you and laughs, try and treat it as an isolated incident. Yes, it will feel horrible and it shouldn't have happened, but other people make situations unpredictable and you can only do your best to minimize disruptions, not do away with them completely.

After any setback, take your time to let your emotions calm down and then try and work out if there's anything you could do to stop it from happening again next time. Try a different class, try outside of school, or practice with your family first. Making mistakes and suffering failures helps you to find the right path to success, and even if it isn't the smoothest journey, the destination is worth it.

Chapter Seven

What's Normal Anyway?

IF YOU ARE ALWAYS trying to be normal, you'll never know how amazing you can be. –Maya Angelou

The term normal is problematic for many reasons, the biggest one being that what is considered normal is constantly changing. It used to be normal that all tv programmes were live, that computers were the size of a large bedroom, and that girls only wore skirts. The reason these things have changed is due to technological and social advancement, pioneered by those people who chose to be not normal.

Because sometimes normal sucks. It literally means something that is usual or expected, not what is best or most beneficial. It used to be normal for everyone to smoke cigarettes—in fact, doctors would even prescribe them for anxiety—and this was only challenged because some researchers decided to challenge the usual behavior. Without people acting against the normal expected behaviors, we also wouldn't have abolished slavery, seen the US become independent from the UK, or invented rock music.

But somewhere along the way, everything got turned around. Instead of teenagers rebelling against society's idea of what is normal, they became obsessed with matching it completely. Not being normal has become such a terrible label that it causes a lot of anxiety among today's teens. A lot of the time, when people say that something isn't normal, they mean they find it surprising, unsettling, disturbing, or weird. This could be because they don't understand it or it doesn't fit into their personal sphere of experience. Adolescents, however, mean that something—or someone—doesn't conform to an idealized view.

Not only do adolescents place a lot of pressure on themselves to match the image of "normal," they're also subject to varying amounts of peer pressure. Peer pressure happens when an individual or a group of people try to convince you to do something because they're doing it and it's perceived as "normal." The funny thing about peer pressure is it can happen passively as well as actively. Trying to match what other groups are doing, without their encouragement, is passive peer pressure. If a friend passes you alcohol at a party and tells you that you need to drink it because that's what people do at parties, they are pressuring you. If you pick up the alcohol yourself because everyone else is drinking it, you are giving in to peer pressure.

Peer pressure and the pressure of societal expectations—even if we are projecting them ourselves—can make the idea of normal incredibly harmful. Look at some of the images we are bombarded with today that show supposedly normal people. There are teenagers wearing expensive outfits, with flawless skin and shiny hair, surrounded by friends, and looking happy. These pictures are in magazines, tv shows, and movies, and they are so prevalent that they have become the normal standard by which every adolescent unfairly judges themselves.

And it's not just the images of teenagers that can be problematic. Movie stars like Chris Evans, Chris Hemsworth, and Henry Cavill are constantly paraded by magazines as having the ideal male physique, and if you want to attract a partner, that's how you should look. But not only is it impossible for teenagers to achieve, no matter how many weights they lift, what the pictures don't tell you is that all three have nearly ended up in the hospital while shooting their superhero movies because they pushed their bodies too far. The role models for a female physique are no better, with Kim Kardashian, Beyonce, and Nikki Minaj all showcasing an impossible hourglass figure, telling teenage girls that small waists are a must-have.

The truth is, no one fits this idea of normal. Teenagers—and adults, because these body types aren't the norm for us either—come in all shapes, sizes, races, genders, and sexualities. There is no normal in the way it's being sold to you. Here is what normal should look like for adolescents:

- It's normal to not like something about the way you look while you're going through puberty.

- It's normal to compare yourself to others.

- It's normal to have unpredictable emotional re-actions to things.

- It's normal to find some things easy and some things difficult.

- It's normal to take some time to figure out who you are and how you fit into this world.

- It's normal to feel different.

When Normal Isn't Normal

Something that's been particularly destructive to the relationship between teenagers and the idea of normal is the invention and worldwide adoption of social media. There are some wonderful things that social media has done—from bringing people together to spreading awareness for a number of important causes—but it has also created a platform where the users create the content and that content can be praised by others. And herein lies the issue. Social media has taken the worst thing about popularity contests and peddled it as the new normal.

Take a look at any celebrity TikTok or Instagram post and I'll bet you they are as carefully scripted, choreographed, and managed as their other public appearances. They might not look like it, but that's the magic of good PR. By passing these posts off as a slice of everyday life, they are distorting the reality of what their followers think is normal. Suddenly, having an immaculately clean and tidy kitchen is "normal." Having a full face of makeup on and your hair perfectly styled, even though you're only lounging around the house in your pajamas, is "normal."

Celebrities are trend setters because we aspire to be like them, even if we don't want to admit it. We copy their clothes and their hairstyles, read the books they recommend, and when they post a video of their "normal" day, we copy that too. But our "normal" day doesn't look the same, so what do we do? We lie.

Social media isn't live, it allows us to rehearse, dress the set, and get into costume. Once you've taken your photo or video, you can edit it completely. Change the filter, erase the bits you don't like, shave an inch off your waist, or you can ditch it completely and take another one. When you post it, you deliver a snapshot of you at your absolute, and often unnatural, best. And people leave positive comments, telling you you're amazing, which means you feel the pressure to post another one that is equally polished.

Where this causes an issue is in real life. In previous chapters, we looked at the biological reasons why teens are more emotional, more insecure, and more focused on what other people think of them than they have been as children. Show a teenager in this state a series of perfect photos and tell them that that's normal and they're going to feel two things: an overwhelming sense of otherness and the instant recognition that everyone else knows they aren't "normal" too.

Deconstructing Perfect

If you were thinking logically—which you can't, because that part of your brain is still under construction—you'd realize that you can't possibly recreate a practiced photo in a real-life situation. Instead, adolescents can go to extremes to try and match up to this media presentation of "normal."

- Getting up extra early in the morning to find the perfect outfit and create flawless makeup for the day at school. Teenagers need between eight and ten hours of sleep every night because the changes to your brain and body are sapping a lot of energy. If you get less sleep than this on a long-term basis, this is called sleep deprivation and it can have some pretty nasty side effects. These include being moody, feeling depressed, difficulty concentrating, and a drop in performance at school (Better Health Channel, n.d.).

- Putting yourself on a restrictive diet to make your figure match the photoshopped images online. It's a natural part of puberty that your body will change shape and gain weight. This is due to shifting fat stores, which your body uses for energy, and the gain of muscle mass. Puberty also causes growth spurts, but if you don't provide your body with enough nutrients to create the new bone, muscle, and organ tissue it needs, you'll end up with problems later on, which could affect your fertility, digestive health, and organ function (Saunders & Smith, 2010).

- Exercising excessively in order to attain a perfect figure. Your body has enough to do during puberty, so if you stress it further by excessive exercising, you're forcing it to choose where to spend its energy. Too much exercise actually has the effect of delaying changes, such as starting to have periods and developing adult muscles. This can also have long-term effects by changing what your pituitary gland thinks is normal, which can lead to a hormonal imbalance (Nemours Children's Health, 2018).

- Pressurizing yourself to look "normal" and do "normal" things. This will raise your stress and anxiety levels throughout the day, as you are constantly checking whether you are upholding the image you want to project. Subjecting your body to high levels of the stress hormone cortisol for long periods of time can lead to a number of serious health conditions, including heart disease and an increased risk of having a stroke. It also makes you more likely to suffer from depression, have trouble sleeping, weight gain, and feel exhausted all the time (Mayo Clinic, 2021

- Neglecting the things you enjoy in order to spend more time appearing "normal." When you spend so much time focusing on something that you don't enjoy, you leave very little time for actually having fun. When you do something you enjoy, your brain releases dopamine and serotonin, which not only make you feel happy, they also play a part in reducing the amount of cortisol in your bloodstream. This helps to reduce the effects of stress and acts as a reset button for your brain (Eske, 2019).

These don't sound like the sort of things that someone should have to do to be perfect. Perfect means that something is as good as it can be, and someone who is making changes that have a negative effect on themselves is not making themselves perfect. In order to be truly perfect, channel your efforts into being the best "you" you can be.

Accepting Our Differences

Society as a whole is beginning to wake up to the damaging effects that our current idea of "normal" can have on adolescents. This means that the depictions of teenagers in the media are evolving to more effectively represent the reality you all see every day. Look at some popular teen movies from the 1990s and 2000s like *Clueless, Cruel Intentions,* and *Mean Girls.* Each film's popularity lasts today and those adults who grew up with these movies remember them fondly, but each film also shows a group of teenagers who either aspire to emulate what they think the popular, normal kids are doing or are those kids. No wonder grown ups are screwed up!

Now take a look at some of the popular movies and series you can watch today that represent your generation in a much more diverse manner. The Netflix series *Sex Education, Stranger Things,* and *Heartstopper* all focus on adolescents who are shown as individuals with their own strengths and personalities. There are very few attempts by any character to sacrifice their own identity to fit in with another group, and when this does happen, it's portrayed as a tragedy rather than the ultimate goal. Instead, they focus on other normal issues that teenagers are dealing with, like questioning your sexuality, making new friends, saving the world, and alien sex fantasies.

Because what is normal anyway? Normal is what is usual, what happens most often. But this is different for every single person on the planet. We are far too diverse to have an expected normal that can possibly include everyone—there are almost 8 billion people on this planet after all. The best you can do is navigate your life according to your own normal. If your normal makes you happy, then great. If it doesn't, then make yourself a new normal. But make sure it is your own and you aren't trying to copy the polished and rehearsed image that someone else is telling you leads to happiness. Because it isn't attainable without a team of stylists and a good editor.

Chapter Eight

Discovering Your True Self

*A*LWAYS BE A FIRST-RATE *version of yourself, instead of a second-rate version of someone else. –Judy Garland*

Adolescence has traditionally been a time of self-discovery where teens take the time to try new things, meet different people, and find out what they enjoy doing. It's the stage of your life when you begin to develop preferences, but that also means learning to get along with other people who don't share them.

It's not a coincidence that this happens now, as puberty forces as many changes on your brain as it does on your body. While this is all going on, it can make everything pretty messy.

It's Update Time!

Your brain is a fascinating organism and is often compared to a computer because of the sheer amount of functions and operations it is capable of carrying out. Not only is it responsible for creating conversation, making decisions, and regulating automated processes like breathing, it also stores all of your memories and your personality. Basically, without your brain, you wouldn't be you and you wouldn't be alive.

If your brain is basically nature's computer, then puberty can be seen as the mother of all updates. We've all suffered from computer issues when installing an update—lagging files, broken links, and the installation of new programs that you didn't necessarily ask for. You go about trying to reset your preferences, redownload your old screensaver, and eventually get used to the changes. Coming out the other side of puberty feels pretty similar.

Rewriting the Network

Your brain works by sending and receiving electrical and chemical signals through transmitters called neurons. (Johns Hopkins Medicine, 2019). The messages your brain sends to your muscles tell them to contract or relax, which makes your body move. The messages your brain receives tell you how it feels, for example, if you're cold or hungry. These signals move really fast because your brain has incredible processing speed. Let's say you accidentally touch a plate that's too hot. Your nerves send signals from your fingers to your brain, telling it that they detected pain. The brain processes these signals and decides on an immediate automated response. It sends signals to your arm muscles telling them to contract and pull your hand away from the plate.

Different sections of your brain are responsible for different processes. In the example above, it would have been the parietal lobe that responded because that's the area of the brain that deals with pain and touch. The parietal lobe is at the back of your brain, just above the occipital lobe, which is responsible for processing what you see. At the front of the brain, you have the temporal lobe where short-term memories hang out and your conversations start. On top of that is the frontal lobe. (Johns Hopkins Medicine, 2019).

The frontal lobe is the area of the brain that is in charge of decision making, movement, and all your personality traits and quirks. It's the part that makes you different from everyone else. Grown ups do most of their thinking with their frontal lobe, which is why it gets the biggest makeover during puberty. New networks and pathways between neurons are made and old ones are pruned back as they become inefficient. But, just like an updating computer program, while all these changes are taking place, you can't always use your frontal lobe in the way you should. So, if teenagers don't always use the rational part of their brain for thinking, where are these decisions rerouted to?

Emotion Central

A lot of teenage thinking takes place in a part of the brain called the amygdala. (Stanford Children's Health, n.d.). There are actually two amygdalas, one on each side of the brain. They're nestled up near the temporal lobe, and they are the hub of your thoughts and emotions. The amygdala is also responsible for regulating the body's reactions to stress and stressful stimuli, as well as housing a lot of dopamine receptors. (Johns Hopkins Medicine, n.d.). This means two things—your responses to stress are heightened, and your urges to feel happy and excited are stronger—and explains why teenagers run from some situations and toward others. If studying for an exam is stressful and hanging with your mates is fun, it's a no-brainer which option you're going to choose because you're thinking with your emotions, not logical reasoning.

In fact, studies show that a lot of typical teenage traits like being rebellious, impulsive, and risk-taking are all caused by the brain's rewiring process (Robson, 2022). The neural pathways between the amygdala and the frontal lobe

116

aren't as well developed as others, so when teenagers have a strong emotional response to something, these signals don't always make it to the frontal lobe for logical processing. When you don't know why you did some-thing, you can legitimately say it's because your brain wasn't thinking of the consequences or long-term results of your actions.

Downloading Personality.exe

Your personality isn't set in stone. Instead, it evolves over the course of your life. Generally speaking, you tend to develop more positive traits—like being nice to people and being able to compromise—as you get older, which is why a lot of adults are better at avoiding and resolving conflict than children and teenagers. Negative qualities you had as a child also tend to be rooted out by interac-tions with your peers and caregivers, meaning very few people grow up maintaining the same levels of selfish-ness or emotional instability as a five year old.

Your teenage years can cause a major bump in the road. During these years—down to the increase in estrogen and testosterone again—personality traits that had been mellowing can once again rear their ugly head. Teenagers generally become less conscientious and more self-serv-ing, which is one of the reasons why adults tend to look down on adolescents. In simple terms, you guys just become less, well, nice.

Spending Your Personality Points

Teenage personality changes aren't all bad though. All those changes firing in your brain are also helping to ignite and develop new characteristics, which will make you an all-round more interesting individual. This is the time in your life when you develop traits that will underpin how you deal with things for the rest of your life. Are you an introvert or an extrovert? Do you feel things or think things through? Can you cope with a sudden change in plan or do you thrive on order?

There's a common misconception that these personality traits will dictate all your future choices in life, such as introverts don't go to parties, work in jobs that aren't customer facing, or will have few friends. This is a very outdated concept and has led to a lot of introverts forcing themselves out of their comfort zone so much that they burn out because of the constant stress. Instead, understanding your personality traits can help you find the best way to manage everything you want to do. Introverts can go to parties, but they may need to leave early, or spend the morning after away from conversation while they recharge their social batteries.

Looking into your personality traits can be a good way to understand why you find something difficult when other people find it easy. You can take a free personality test online at www.16personalities.com, which will provide you with a detailed breakdown of why you act the way you do and what this means about you. Remember, though, your personality is still in flux and will be for many years. A personality test taken now will probably give you a different result than one you take in five, ten, and twenty years' time.

Making the Most of You

Your personality is one of the biggest reasons why people will want to be friends with you and spend time with you. When you were a child, you made your friends based on a number of factors, which were often out of your control. They were kids who lived in your street, who were in your class, or who had caregivers that were friends with yours, and that was fine. Children are much more accepting of other people and less likely to form intense feelings of dislike toward one another, unless there is a distinct cause, such as bullying behavior.

Teenagers, however, are much more discerning, and this can be devastating for existing friendships. Because teenage friendships run much deeper, some of the bonds you made with people from your childhood will become superficial and that might mean that people drift apart. While this is perfectly natural and completely okay, it can feel upsetting if your friends move on with other people and you don't. This can happen at any time, but it's especially common when starting at high school.

Suddenly, there are hundreds of new people to meet and a wider pool of friends to choose from is going to increase the likelihood that you find people you have something in common with.

Being left behind by friends can make you feel unworthy. Try and remind yourself that you did nothing wrong and that you will find people out there who choose you; not because you're local or their parents have arranged a playdate, but because they think you're interesting, amazing, and fun to be around.

What Makes You Different?

During adolescence your brain becomes obsessed with comparing you to everyone else and trying to convince you that you need to fit in with a group. The problem comes when you are more concerned with fitting into any group than finding the right group. Yes, being one of the popular kids looks like fun, but if you have to hide parts of your personality and drop hobbies that you enjoy, is it really going to be worth it? Some people would say yes, but I think the majority of you are sensible enough to realize that you don't make real, lasting friends by pretending to be something you're not. Instead of trying to be like everyone else, you should be embracing your differences.

I'm sure you can reel off a dozen things you feel make you different from everyone else, but do they all sound negative? It's so much easier to feel badly about yourself than it is to feel positively, especially when your mind and body are going through a lot of changes that you aren't necessarily enjoying. Instead, try thinking: What unique qualities do I have to offer that no one else does? These are the reasons why people will want to be friends with you, so you need to show them off.

When you were a child, you knew what you liked and what you were good at without any second-guessing. You would proudly declare to everyone you met if you could belch the loudest, jump the highest, or knew how to craft each object in *Minecraft* from memory. These are all excellent qualities, but for some reason, they don't seem to be as important to other people now that your age is made up of double figures.

Luckily, you are a multifaceted human being and there will be plenty of other things you are good at and many positive qualities you have that will make others enjoy spending time with you. But how can you remind yourself what these are? Try thinking back to times when previous friends or family members have complimented you. Did they like that you always planned fun activities? Maybe you used to bake your own snacks to take to sleepovers. Perhaps you were always supportive and encouraged people to try new things and celebrated their successes, no matter how small. If your self-esteem is too low at the moment to find your own positives, ask the people in your family what they like best about you. You could even look through old report cards for encouraging comments from teachers. Younger siblings might say that you're fun to play with, while older ones might like that you respect their privacy. The adults in your life will recognise qualities like kindness, helpfulness, and thoughtfulness.

Reframing Negative Views

It's also worth thinking about some of the things you dislike about yourself or qualities you view as a fault. This is your view, but there are plenty of ways some of these negatives could be viewed by others as a positive. For example, you hate that you take so long over your work. What other people seem to be able to do in half an hour often takes you two. It's because you need it to be perfect and you panic if it's anything less. This can be a positive thing because it means you fully commit to a project, and therefore, will be likely to fully commit to a friendship too. Somebody out there will be delighted that you are always there for them and they will describe you as reliable and steadfast.

Reframing things like this is a skill that is well worth learning, but it can take a lot of practice. Here are a few other common negative thoughts that you can reframe, so you can see more examples of how it works.

Negative Quality	Positive Reframing	Why Friends Like You
I can't control my reactions. I'm too unpredictable and emotional.	Getting emotional means I'm passionate and caring.	I will always stick up for my friends when they are wronged.
I'm not good at or interested in popular things.	I am good at other things, which are also valuable.	I introduce people to new interests and experiences.
Every time I try something new, I'm never as good as the others.	I'm open to new experiences and therefore, more likely to find my perfect hobby or subject.	We can improve together and they might enjoy helping me learn.
I get really anxious every time I have to speak up in class, so I don't say much.	I consider my words carefully because I know the impact they can have.	When I do say something, it's often important, well thought out, and good advice.

Putting Yourself Out There

Once you've identified the best bits about your person-ality—the amazing things you can offer that any friends would be lucky to benefit from—how do you let other people see them? You can't exactly paint them on your back and parade around school like a walking advert.

Instead, you have to demonstrate them in practice and show your peers what you have to offer. Here's an example:

You've identified that one of your positive qualities is your generosity. You enjoy making others happy by giving them what they need, whether that's an actual object or just your time. You decide you're going to watch out for times at school where you can showcase this.

- In Spanish class, you give a spare pencil to Iris-Helen and tell her to keep it because you have plenty.

- You stay behind after art class to help Marc clean up the paints he knocked over. It was an accident, but the teacher didn't believe him and made him stay as a punishment for messing around, which is something he is known for doing. He appreciates your support and you both talk about your projects while you tidy.

- The drama society is looking for volunteers to help with their latest play. You can't stand the thought of being in the spotlight, but you enjoy art and are good at organizing, so you put your name down to help with the set and the props.

- You're reading a book during your lunch break and Chantal mentions that she's read the first one in the series. You offer to lend her yours when you're done with it because you know she'll enjoy it.

Each of the above actions showcases generosity in a way that makes a connection with another person or group of people. They also leave each interaction in a positive way, opening a door for the other person to respond. If you're not comfortable trying to initiate conversations with small talk, these small acts of kindness open you up and let other people know they can approach you instead. Marc might say hello next time he passes you in the corridor. Iris-Helen might choose you as a work partner for the next class. Chantal might return your book and invite you to join her book club. The drama club people might love your set designs and make sure you get an invite to all of their social events.

When people give you the advice that you should put yourself out there, this is usually what they mean. Rather than forcing yourself to show up in places where you don't feel comfortable, always make sure you show off all the positive qualities you have that will make you an excellent friend. It's like a café putting its best cakes on show in the window—the display attracts people and those who are really interested will go inside. If you put your best qualities on display, the people who care about those parts of you will make contact.

Chapter Nine

Leaving the Friendzone: Taking the Relationship Further

*T*HERE IS NO LOVE *like the first!* –Nicholas Sparks

It's an expectation of adolescence that you'll want to get involved with dating, relationships, love, and sex. After all, puberty is usually defined as a sexual awakening because the hormones testosterone and estrogen have such a profound effect on your reproductive organs. While this can be damagingly dismissive of the other changes you are going through, it's not altogether incorrect. The majority of teenagers find that sex suddenly enters the agenda in a number of different ways. It appears on the school curriculum and you get subjected to a range of lessons that break it down to its biological functions to others involving realistic models and step-by-step instructions for applying condoms.

Here is where another "normal" assumption can cause confusion. Not only is there considerably more information available about "normal" sexual progression, which ignores or marginalizes LGBT+ teens, but the fact that everyone starts talking about it can lead you to assume that that means everyone is doing it, when this is probably quite far from the truth. Grown ups, in their misguided but admirable attempts to help out, will throw a bunch of information at teenagers because that's much easier and less embarrassing than sitting down with you and actually talking about stuff.

Discussing sex and dating with your caregivers is a non-starter for many teenagers. Either you've pulled away from them during adolescence, which means that a conversation of such an intimate nature would be uncomfortable, or you're aware that your understanding and experience is taking a different path to theirs. School employees are often limited in what they can say because they're bound by the school's policy. For example, if your school teaches abstinence, then teachers cannot discuss birth control with you, so you'll probably turn to your friends and peers for information and advice. But they're new to this too. It can feel like you're all trying to navigate an obstacle course in a dark room.

However, as we've established in previous chapters, teenagers are highly sensitive to what others think of them, and no one wants to feel that they're being judged for something they have or haven't done. If someone asked you if you had a partner, and you felt they would judge you for saying no, even if it was the truth, would you lie?

Dating is a new experience for all teenagers, and nobody wants to feel like they are falling behind the curve. If your peers tell you they're all having sex and have dated multiple people—hopefully not at the same time—while you can't even bring yourself to talk to the person you have a crush on, it's going to make you feel inadequate, even if it's not true.

I pointed out in chapter one that puberty usually—and there are exceptions—begins between the ages of 8 and 14. It's entirely down to your biological programming when your body starts the process and there's nothing you can do to change it. Puberty itself can also last between two and five years. How good are you at calculations? There's a huge range of experiences possible because of those statistics; yet another reason to shy away from the idea of "normal."

If you start puberty at age 13, you are going to be developmentally behind someone who started at 9. It's highly possible that their body and brain chemistry has finished all the changes it's going to make before yours has even started. So, if they look more grown up than you, this is why. If they've figured out who they are attracted to but you've not even started to think about anyone else in that way, this is why. Their experience of puberty shouldn't influence yours. It's like meeting someone at the airport who is on their way home from a holiday when you are just setting off. They're done with their trip, but yours is just beginning.

Figuring Stuff Out

Remember, there is no normal time to start dating, and no normal way to do it. Write it on a post-it note above your mirror if you have to because it's probably the most important bit of advice I can pass on. Adolescence is a time of great change and while that change is happening, you might want to experiment and find out what you like, or you might want to wait until it's all over before embarking on your first forays into the dating world. The most important thing is to only do what you are comfortable with and never do something you are uncomfortable with because someone asks you to or expects you to.

As your body responds to increased levels of sex hormones—testosterone and estrogen— you may start to experience new feelings toward other people. These will fall into two categories: romantic feelings and sexual feelings. It's important to note the difference between the two because many people experience them differently.

Sexual feelings are usually linked to finding someone attractive and will produce a bodily response, which includes increased blood flow to your genitals as well as increased blood pressure, heart rate, body temperature and a change in your breathing. ("Arousal," n.d.). Many adolescents enjoy these new feelings because they are exciting, but others find them unpleasant or inconvenient. Those who don't experience them at all may identify as asexual or on the ace spectrum—a term for all the people who don't experience sexual attraction, who only experience it occasionally, or whose experience of sexual attraction is varying.

Romantic feelings can manifest as a desire to spend increased time with someone, as an intense emotional response to your relationship, or feeling a deep connection with someone. This doesn't need to include wanting to have a physical relationship, and there are asexual people who have romantic feelings toward others. Some people don't experience romantic feelings and they may identify as aromantic or on the aro spectrum—a term for all the people who don't experience romantic attraction, who only experience it occasionally, or whose experience of romantic attraction is varying. ("List of LGBTQ+ terms," n.d.).

Who you feel romantic and sexual feelings toward is decided by your romantic and sexual orientation. These do not need to be the same, although it is unusual for there to be no overlap. Some people are attracted to others of the same gender identity, some are attracted to people of a different gender identity, and others are attracted to all gender identities. Even people who identify as asexual may identify with a romantic orientation, even though they don't experience sexual feelings in the same direction.

During adolescence, it's normal to experience confusion about your orientation, to feel attraction toward a diverse range of people, or to have your orientation change and evolve overtime. You are learning to process new feelings with no reference points in your previous experiences, which is going to mean a lot of trial and error.

Partners Are People Too

If you've decided you would like to dip your toe into the dating pool, that's great! Having the confidence to seek a deeper connection with another person is wonderful. Remember, it also takes a lot of confidence to say that you're not ready yet, so if that's you or you get that response from someone you ask out, make sure you respect that decision.

How do you go about finding that special someone? Your best resources for meeting new people you could develop an attraction to are existing friends. They can introduce you to their other friends from different schools, the members of their sports team, even friends of their siblings. The more people you meet, the more likely you are to find someone that catches your eye and makes you want to get to know them more deeply.

All of the information in this book about how to make friends by showing off your best qualities, being interested in what others have to say, and overcoming some of the roadblocks thrown up by anxiety is also excellent advice for getting to know someone you have romantic or sexual feelings for. Isn't that great news? All the work you've already put in has a second function; you just need the right person to test it out on. When you find them, start a conversation like you would with anyone else. Ask questions about them and listen to their responses. Is their body language relaxed? Remember to make eye contact and smile to help them relax.

But before you start doodling their name in hearts and planning to run off into the sunset together, it's important to remember that your feelings might not be reciprocated. Rejection is as much a part of dating as the cinema trips, kissing, and hand holding. Some teenagers are willing to be open-minded about who they date, whereas others will have a very specific list or requirements that they need fulfilled in order to be comfortable with someone else. There's no shame in rejection and it doesn't reflect badly on you as a person; it just means that they didn't have the same feelings for you as you had for them.

It's a Date!

Once you've met someone and mutually agreed that you like each other enough to go out on a date, what next? The odds are that you have met and got along well because you have something in common, so why not arrange to do something that you'll both enjoy? Try not to be rigid in your ideas; if you like hiking, but they aren't as active, it isn't doomed. Perhaps you could organize something like a short walk around a park and a picnic.

It's a good idea to plan an activity that allows you to talk and get to know each other better. Going to the movies can be fun, but your options for chatting are limited. However, if you follow the movie with a hot chocolate and cake at a local cafe, you're building on the enjoyment of the film and giving you both a chance to talk. In fact, organizing an exciting activity before a calm chat has many benefits, such as:

- It gives you both a shared experience to talk about. Knowing that you don't have to search for a topic of conversation can be a huge relief and alleviate some of the butterflies you might be feeling.

- Enjoying an activity will release the happy hormones in your brain. Your brain will associate this feeling with the person you are on a date with, meaning that you are more likely to want to spend time with them again—and them with you.

- Having a structured activity can distract you from feeling nervous. A conversation can meander, but when you sit down to watch a movie, pick up a bowling ball, or enter an escape room, you know what to expect from the activity. Doing something where you feel comfortable, because it is predictable, helps you to relax.

If your date suggests doing something you haven't tried before, it's entirely your decision whether you say yes or no. But remember, your choice should be governed by whether or not you feel comfortable. For example, they suggest going to a climbing wall at their local gym, but you don't feel comfortable because you are worried that too many strangers would be watching you and you don't feel confident climbing. If you agree to go, your experience of the date, and of this person, is going to be tainted by the stress and anxiety you experience in the run up to the event and then during the date itself.

If you say no, you don't need to explain in great detail; it is okay to just say it's not something you fancy doing and suggest an alternative. Choosing what to do together should be a discussion, not a dictation! Likewise, if your date rejects your initial suggestion, make sure you respect their decision and don't push them for an explanation. You are still getting to know each other, and showing that you can respect each other's boundaries from the start is a great foundation for a relationship.

Chapter Ten

Translating the Secret Code of Body Language and Nonverbal Communication

I CAN READ YOUR body language like a conversation. –Dom Kennedy

You will have already learned a couple of things about body language and nonverbal communication in the previous chapters, but it's such an important method of communicating that it deserves its own space.

As a detective, I spent decades of my life in the interview room, where reading a subject's body language was a necessary superpower. Very few guilty people give themselves up immediately, at least not verbally, but by assessing how they sat, listening to their tone of voice, and watching their facial expressions, I was able to read a lot more than they wanted me to.

The science of body language research goes back to the 1960s, when a well-respected figure in the scientific community, Professor Albert Mehrabian designed a series of experiments to look more closely at how humans communicate. (The British Library, 2015). Mehrabian stands out because, despite being a professor of psychology, he originally completed a bachelors and a masters in engineering. Having this background in a subject that requires all theories to be properly tested and backed up with substantial research meant that he dedicated a lot of his time to developing ways to measure and quantify human behavior and reactions.

The 7–38–55 Rule

Mehrabian proposed that there are three core elements that make up the way we convey meaning through speech: our facial expressions, the tone of voice we use, and finally, the words themselves. (The British Library, 2015). If one or more of these elements is missing, we struggle to work out what is really being said. Imagine a computer program that reads out your text messages. With such an expressionless tone of voice, would you be able to tell whether "yeah, it's totally amazing, so glad I came," was sincere or sarcastic?

For his first experiment, Mehrabian showed a group of students a series of photographs of women pulling different expressions. They were a mixture of positive, negative, and neutral expressions. They were designed to reflect the expression you might see on the face of someone you're talking to, depending on whether they liked you, disliked you, or didn't have an opinion. He asked the students to choose which photograph fitted into which category.

Then, for his second experiment, Mehrabian asked the same group of students to listen to some voice recordings. They all said the same word but in different tones. These were also designed to convey liking, disliking, or a neutral opinion. The students were again asked to say which voice recording fitted into which category. The students correctly identified the facial expressions with more accuracy than the vocal tone. (The British Library, 2015).

Mehrabian conducted more experiments, this time adding one that asked students to decide if the tone of voice matched the words used. At the end of the experiments, he found out that people were able to read the facial expressions most accurately, then the tone of voice, and lastly the words that were spoken. With some mathematical wizardry, he came up with a formula, which became the 7–38–55 rule. This means that our understanding of what someone is saying is relayed 7% by their words, 38% by the vocal tone they use, and 55% by their expression on their face.

Mehrabian's research is often woefully misquoted. For one thing, it looked specifically at feelings and whether the person you're talking to likes you or not. People have taken his findings and applied them to communication in general, and while that isn't what the rule was designed for, it still has some interesting implications.

One thing Mehrabian's study was really good at showing is that, when two of these elements contradict each other, you give more weight to what someone's body language is saying than their words. In some instances, what comes out of your mouth and what you communicate through your body language may be two totally different things. If you say one thing, but your body language says something else, whoever you're talking to is going to feel confused. For instance, if you say yes while shaking your head, or tell them you want to chat but then keep looking at your watch or toward the door, they won't know what you're trying to say. Since body language is a natural, unconscious language, and you can choose whether you use words that under normal circumstances broadcast your true feelings and intentions, they'll likely choose the nonverbal message. It's this knowledge that I used to my advantage when coaxing confessions out of criminals.

Essentially, people tend to trust nonverbal cues more than they do verbal ones, especially when the meaning between the two doesn't line up. Therefore, because body language is seen as trustworthy, it will have one of the following effects:

- It will emphasize or strengthen what you are saying. Tell someone you love them while holding their hands and gazing into their eyes, as these cues will back up your words with a deeper meaning.

- It can contradict the message you're attempting to convey, letting whoever you're talking to know that you may not be telling the truth. If you tell someone you love them without eye contact and in a flat tone of voice, they'll be able to tell that your heart isn't in it.

A Fourth Element?

There is another factor that Mehrabian didn't include in his experiment that we use every day to help us decipher communications. Look back at my example text message in the third paragraph. When placed in context, would you now be able to tell if it was sarcastic or sincere? Applying context to a situation is vital in helping us to interpret everything, including nonverbal communications. A good example is to look at a common pose that you'll see people pulling everyday, like arms crossed over the torso. This action can have a number of different meanings, depending on what else is going on. Here are a few examples for you:

- Arms crossed on a subway might just indicate politeness, as they don't want to accidentally take up someone else's space, or it might indicate they're feeling uncomfortable with the number of people and are trying to put a barrier between themselves and the world. The first person would have a relaxed facial expression whereas the second person would look stiff and avoid eye contact.

- Crossed arms could mean someone has received bad news and are literally giving themselves a comforting hug. Crossing the arms simulates protection, and being straight over the heart usually implies emotions are involved. If the person also grips their biceps they're showing extreme discomfort. Recently, experts have also concluded that crossing your arms can also just be a sign of getting comfortable, so without other context or signals it might not have any deeper meaning at all. (Jung, n.d.).

- If someone has crossed their arms and balled their hands into fists, back away slowly! They might have felt a bit defensive, but now they're full on angry. Sometimes this happens when no one has interpreted their crossed arms as a sign to leave them alone, and as their discomfort increases, they become more desperate for a way out of the situation.

- People who are feeling defiant often cross their arms as a way to let you know that they are putting up a barrier and you won't get through. This is accompanied by them leaning back, as if inviting you to try and invade the space they've just blocked off. I saw this one many times across an interview table, and you'll often see it from the bullies at school.

Body is Your First Language

What makes body language really interesting is that you use it to communicate from the moment you're born. Most babies smile intentionally for the first time at around two months old, up until then it's usually because they have gas! They smile because they're happy to see their family members. It's why a game of peek-a-boo is so much fun for the adults too; it triggers that beautiful response time after time and lets them know that their baby is happy.

As time goes on, the signals that you give out become more refined to match the increasing array of emotions you can feel. A wrinkled nose to signal disgust, a frown for disapproval, bouncing arms and legs to show excitement. What's also amazing is the speed at which your caregivers learn to read your body language. They'll know when you're about to cry, when you're too tired to cope with a situation, and even when you're about to soil your undergarments. It seems that reading body language is as natural to us as speaking it.

Autotranslate Installed as Standard

Even now, as teenagers, you give out hundreds of body language signals throughout the day. You might change the rate at which your eyes blink, the tilt of your head and neck, the way you lick your lips, or how you press your tongue into your cheek. And those are just the ones you have control over. Your body automatically dilates your pupils when looking at someone you're attracted to. It changes the color of your skin, making you blush if you're embarrassed or turn pale if you're scared. You might not realize it, but you are also constantly processing the signals you receive from other people.

Picture a typical day walking down a busy corridor at school. You'll notice who to avoid by picking up on their signals. Maybe it's the troublemaker leaning against the lockers with his arms crossed and a scowl on his face—a clear sign that he's waiting for someone to pick a fight with. Or the girl with her head down and arms thrust stiffly into her pockets—both could be defensive and aggressive signals, letting people know there'll be consequences for not leaving her alone. So, you walk a little closer to the group who are chatting and laughing together, big smiles on their faces and their shoulders relaxed, because if you accidentally knock into them, it won't register as a big deal.

Fine Tune Your Skills

There is no tried and tested list of nonverbal signals I can give you that I can say will 100% let you know how people are feeling. Unless you're dealing with a baby, then it's pretty straightforward. In an interview situation, I would have to learn a suspect's individual cues that would tell me when they were anxious, lying, or about to throw a punch. How did I do it? Years of practice and a lot of experience. By letting them relax at the start of an interview, I could watch for what changed as I started to ask more probing questions. When I got a reaction, I knew that was the right button to press.

Reading the signals of people you know well is even easier. Because you've spent a lot of time around them, you have an incredible wealth of knowledge of their behaviors in all different contexts. Knowing what your friends look and sound like at their most relaxed will help you spot when they're feeling stressed, anxious, worried, or unhappy—or if they are trying to hide something from you. Remember, the studies into nonverbal communication all started because Mehrabian wanted to see if people picked up when there was a disparity between someone's tone (unconscious) and their words (conscious). When something is out of sync, you can guarantee you're being lied to.

Studying the different nonverbal cues that your friends and classmates give off will help you to improve how well you understand and use your own nonverbal signals. This means you can be certain that you're saying what you really mean, which will help you to connect better with others and build stronger, more rewarding relationships. Your nonverbal communication cues—the way you listen, look, move, and react—tell the person you're communicating with whether or not you care about them and what they're saying, something that is really important in a good friendship. If your friends aren't giving you these signals, it could be a sign that they're a bad friend or they could have something important or upsetting on their mind—check for context again! Either way, you can tell them you know something is up and ask what they're really thinking about.

Did you enjoy the book?

Please take a moment to leave a review, as it can greatly benefit the book's visibility. Your review not only supports me, the author (for which I am eternally grateful), but also helps guide other readers searching for a similar book to discover it and has the potential to help someone benefit from the advice offered in this book.

Thank you, your support is greatly appreciated

Kev

References

AMERICAN PSYCHOLOGICAL ASSOCIATION. (2022, August). *Anxiety.* https://www.apa.org/topics/anxiety

Arousal. (n.d.). https://www.plannedparenthood.org/learn/sex-pleasure-and-sexual-dysfunction/sex-and-pleasure/arousal

Better Health Channel. (n.d.). *Teenagers and sleep.* https://www.betterhealth.vic.gov.au/health/healthyliving/teenagers-and-sleep

Child Helpline International. (n.d.). *Find your local child helpline.* https://childhelplineinternational.org/helplines/

Childline. (n.d.). *Want to feed good.* https://www.childline.org.uk/

Cincinnati Children's. (n.d.). *Cognitive development.* https://www.cincinnatichildrens.org/health/c/cognitive

Day, V. (2022, July 23). *Positive Social Skills for Teens.* DreamWorld Publications.

Dowshen, S. (2015). *Everything you wanted to know about puberty.* TeensHealth. https://kidshealth.org/en/teens/puberty.html

Eske, J. (2019, August 19). *Dopamine vs. serotonin: similarities, differences, and relationship.* Medical News Today. https://www.medicalnewstoday.com/articles/326090

Fleming, W. (2022, June 20). *50+ Awesome and inspirational quotes for teenagers.* Parenting Teens and Tweens. https://parentingteensandtweens.com/inspirational-quotes-for-teenagers/

45 open-ended questions for kids and parents to initiate conversation. (2020, June 17). Gathered Again. https://gatheredagain.com/open-ended-questions-for-kids/

Frank. (n.d.). *Honest information about drugs.* https://talktofrank.com/

Harvard Health Publishing. (2020, July 7). *Exercising to relax.* Harvard Health Publishing. https://www.health.harvard.edu/staying-healthy/exercising-to-relax

Hooper, B., Moor, D. D., & Siracusa, E. (2022, October 12). *Animal friendships are surprisingly like our own.* The Conversation. https://theconversation.com/animal-friendships-are-surprisingly-like-our-own-188120

Hughes, J. K. (2020, August 28). *Flip the script - a guide to imaginal exposure*. Justin K. Hughes. https://www.justinkhughes.com/jog/flip-the-script-a -guide-to-imaginal-exposure/

Jarrett, C. (2018, June 11). *How our teenage years shape our personalities*. BBC. https://www.bbc.com/future/article/20180608-ho w-our-teenage-years-shape-our-personalities

Johns Hopkins Medicine. (n.d.). *Brain anatomy and how the brain works*. https://www.hopkinsmedicine.org/heal th/conditions-and-diseases/anatomy-of-the-brain

Jung, A. (n.d.). *Are crossed arms rude? 8 secrets your body reveals about you*. Reader's Digest. https://www.readersdigest.com.au/culture/are-crossed -arms-rude-8-secrets-your-body-language-reveals-abou t-you

Kennedy, D. (2011, June 28). *When You See Love*. The Administration MP.

Khurana, S. (2019, January 21). *Young love quotes*. ThoughtCo. https://www.thoughtco.com/young-love-q uotes-2832643

Lewis, Tanika. (2022, April 12). *What does romantic attraction feel like?* WoC Therapy. https://woctherapy.com/what-does-romantic-attraction

-feel-like/#:~:text=Romantical%20feelings%20can%20be%20described,be%20of%20a%20sexual%20nature

List of LGBTQ+ terms. (n.d.). https://www.stonewall.org.uk/list-lgbtq-terms

Mandel, L. (2017, March 8). *Why we need friends, according to a scientist.* https://www.thefader.com/2017/03/08/science-of-friendship

Mayo Clinic. (2018, December 10). *5 tips to manage stress.* https://www.mayoclinichealthsystem.org/hometown-health/speaking-of-health/5-tips-to-manage-stress

Mayo Clinic. (2021, July 8). *Chronic stress puts your health at risk.* https://www.mayoclinic.org/healthy-lifestyle/stress-management/in-depth/stress/art-20046037

Mind. (n.d.). *Useful contacts - for 11-18 year olds.* https://www.mind.org.uk/information-support/for-children-and-young-people/useful-contacts/

Morgan, N., & Cassidy, C. (2017). *The teenage guide to friends.* Walker Books And Subsidiaries.

Nemours Children's Health (2018). *Compulsive exercise for teens.* https://kidshealth.org/en/teens/compulsive-exercise.html

Nemours Children's Health. (n.d.). *Hygiene basics.* https://kidshealth.org/Nemours/en/teens/hygiene-basics.html

NHS Choices. (n.d.). *Causes - acne*. https://www.nhs.uk/conditions/acne/causes/

NHS. (n.d.). *Early or delayed puberty*. https://www.nhs.uk/conditions/early-or-delayed-puberty/

NHS. (n.d.). *Talking to your teenager*. https://www.nhs.uk/mental-health/children-and-young-adults/advice-for-parents/talk-to-your-teenager/

Oro House Recovery Centers. (2021, December 14). *33 famous people and celebrities with social anxiety disorders*. https://www.ororecovery.com/9-famous-people-celebrities-with-social-anxiety-disorders/

Patient. (n.d.). *Surviving adolescence*. https://patient.info/childrens-health/surviving-adolescence

Public School Review. (n.d.). *Average public school student size*. https://www.publicschoolreview.com/average-school-size-stats/national-data

ReachOut. (n.d.). *What makes a good friend?* https://au.reachout.com/articles/what-makes-a-good-friend

Robson, D. (2022, September 7). *The biggest myths of the teenage brain*. BBC. https://www.bbc.com/future/article/20220823-what-really-goes-on-in-teens-brains

Russell, K. (n.d.). *Why teenagers don't talk to their parents*. Peaceful Parents Confident

Kids. http://peacefulparentsconfidentkids.com/2015/0
2/teenagers-dont-talk-to-their-parents/

Saunders, J., & Smith, T. (2010). *Malnutrition: causes
and consequences.* https://doi.org/10.7861/clinmedicine
.10-6-624

South China Morning Post. (2022, March 20). *Chris
Hemsworth's fitness transformation into Thor – but is it
actually   healthy?*
https://www.scmp.com/magazines/style/celebrity/articl
e/3171005/chris-hemsworths-fitness-transformation-th
or-he-follows

Stanford Medicine Children's Health. (n.d.). *Understanding the teen brain.* https://www.stanfordchildrens.org/en
/topic/default?id=understanding-the-teen-brain-1-3051

The British Library. (2015). *Albert Mehrabian.* https://ww
w.bl.uk/people/albert-mehrabian

UNICEF.   (2018,   February   23).   *The   adolescent   brain: a   second   window   of   opportuni-
ty.* https://www.unicef-irc.org/article/1750-the-adolesce
nt-brain-a-second-window-of-opportunity.html

Walker, B. F. (2021). *Social anxiety relief for teens: a
step-by-step CBT guide to feel confident and comfortable in
any situation.* Instant Help.

WebMD Editorial Contributors. (n.d.). *Signs of a bad friend*. WebMD. https://www.webmd.com/balance/signs-bad-friend

Wilding, M. (2018, November 17). *Please stop telling me to leave my comfort zone*. The Guardian. https://www.theguardian.com/us-news/2018/nov/16/comfort-zone-mental-health

Young Minds. (n.d.). *You are not alone.* https://www.youngminds.org.uk/

Resources

THIS BOOK HAS COVERED a lot of different topics and you may find that you want to investigate further. This page contains some websites you might find useful.

Child Helpline International is an organization that collects and coordinates information from children's charities all over the world. Their website can help you find a charity phone line in your country so that you can talk to a trained volunteer.

https://childhelplineinternational.org/helplines/

Mental Health Europe has a comprehensive list of websites and helplines designed to help with mental health problems, including stress, anxiety, panic attacks, hearing voices, and having suicidal thoughts. It has the most information for UK users, but many other European countries are also supported.

www.mhe-sme.org/library/youth-helplines/

The National Alliance on Mental Illness (NAMI) is a US-based organization. Their website is full of links and resources for teens and young adults, including information on how to talk to your caregivers about mental illness.

https://www.nami.org/Your-Journey/Kids-Teens-and-Young-Adults

Marie Stopes International is a charity dedicated to providing reproductive healthcare and advice in 37 countries. They aim to educate people about their choices in a non-judgemental environment.

https://www.msichoices.org/

Mermaids is a UK-based charity that offers advice and support to gender-diverse, transgender, and nonbinary children, teenagers, and their families. Their website is loaded with great resources for anyone questioning their identity.

https://mermaidsuk.org.uk/

In the US, the National Center for Transgender Equality offers resources, blog posts, and links for transgender adults and teens.

https://transequality.org/issues/youth-students

The Trevor Project is a US-based resource for young people questioning their sexuality. Although their helplines are U.S. numbers, their website includes an international, members-only community hub called TrevorSpace, which includes a moderated forum, resources, and clubs where you can explore your sexuality and identity among friends.

www.thetrevorproject.org/

Allsorts Youth Project provides resources and organizes group sessions for LGBT+ young people and their families. Their website is full of leaflets with tips on coming out, information on dealing with your sexuality as a person of color, a podcast, and even reading recommendations.

www.allsortsyouth.org.uk/

If you found that the exercises in this book helped you and you want to explore some more, this page from Therapist Aid has a number of free worksheets you can use to explore your negative thoughts and start reprogramming your thinking.

www.therapistaid.com/therapy-worksheets/cbt/adolescents

About the Author

H AVING A STARK CHOICE of fighting teens on the city streets or helping them find their way in life, Kev Chilton knew which way he wanted to go!

For most of his working life, he was an inner-city cop and detective, concentrating on murder, gun crime, and other serious offences.

However, he joined the police as a 16-year-old cadet and early in his career, he was tasked with helping young offenders, which quickly became his speciality. He noticed that by simply listening to the problems young people were concerned with, the majority were prepared to listen to him back. He built trusting relationships with most, who were happy to listen to and act on his advice. Many responded positively, and they moved confidently into adulthood.

Throughout his police service, he arranged youth clubs, attended schools where he gave talks and maintained an open-door policy, encouraging any young person with a problem to approach him privately afterwards. He also set up and operated specialist juvenile squads geared towards helping those who had gone off the rails. The results were excellent, and he was never happier in his job than when he could redirect a young person's life onto the right path.

It was a fulfilling time in his life, and it helped him understand the constantly evolving challenges teenagers face as they transition to adulthood. More specifically, as times change, so do the needs and circumstances of young people. Choosing the path of mentorship over the chaos of city streets, he has dedicated his journey to helping teenagers, steering them away from conflict and towards a brighter future.

Today, he is proud to utilise his extensive experience to make a positive impact. He is particularly attuned to the unique issues that young people are currently grappling with, and one of his main goals is to bridge the gap between them and the adults in their lives.

Through this series of his guidebooks for teens, Chilton has become an international, award-winning author, and a beacon of support for teenagers and the adults regularly involved with teens.

Today he lives in a converted barn in the beautiful East Kent countryside where family, walking and writing are a big part of his life, and can be reached at :

https://kevchilton.com

STAY IN TOUCH

Join our Newsletter <u>School 'n Cool</u> and become part of an amazing community, offering valuable content for Teens, Parents, Teachers

https://kevchilton.com/contact

https://kevchilton.com/contact

Teens' Guide Series

E VERYTHING A TEENAGER NEEDS to tackle the significant challenges and opportunities of adolescence can be found within this series. From friendships and mental health issues to finding employment, managing finances, and developing adult skills, these five books offer practical guidance for teenagers to navigate these crucial years with resilience and strength.

The Teens' Guide Series of books has everything you'll ever need to navigate your teens.

Teens' Guide Book Series

Book Two

Teens' Guide to Dating

Are you a teen looking to build healthy relationships, set boundaries, and stay safe while dating online or offline? *Teen's Guide to Dating* is here to help you.

Dating can feel overwhelming, whether you're navigating crushes, breakups, or looking after your own safety. Learn how to find the right partner, create meaningful connections, and stay safe. Inside, you'll discover:

·How to know you're ready to date and build confidence
·Ways to set boundaries, get consent, and confidently communicate your needs
·Tips for LGBT+ dating and different stages of relationships
·Safe sex practices, conflict resolution, and handling breakups

Teen's Guide to Dating gives you the tools to not only enjoy your relationship but also become the best version of yourself. Ready to start your journey? Read now!

Book Three

Teens' Guide to Health & Mental Wellness

Do you ever feel overwhelmed, wondering why life affects you more than your friends? Your feelings are valid, and *Teen's Guide to Self-Care and Wellness* will help you understand and manage them.

Life's stresses can take a toll, but with the right tools, you can navigate them effectively. In this guide, you'll learn to:

·Identify negative mental health indicators
·Master the key ingredients for mental wellness
·Use physical strategies to improve mental health
·Provide first aid for anxiety and depression
·Build your own personal wellness toolbox

Learning to manage stress now will make life easier as you grow. Start your journey to wellness with this guide today!

Book Four

Teens' Guide to Financial Independence

Are you a teen seeking financial independence or a parent wanting to guide your teen? *Teen's Guide to Financial Independence* is your go-to resource for building a successful career and managing your money with confidence.

This comprehensive guide will teach you essential skills for employment and wealth-building. Whether you're just starting or need guidance, this book will be your companion throughout. Inside you'll learn how to:

Prepare for the world of work and apply for various jobs
·Create a compelling resume and excel in interviews
·Master budgeting, avoid scams, and handle credit cards wisely
·Balance work and life, and plan for university expenses
·Understand investing, saving, and hidden fees

Start to manage **your** finances and secure **your** future, now!

https://kevchilton.com/books

Made in the USA
Middletown, DE
19 November 2024

65041370R00099